Mike Schmidt

ALSO BY WILLIAM C. KASHATUS

Connie Mack's '29 Triumph:
The Rise and Fall of the Philadelphia Athletics Dynasty
(McFarland, 1999)

A Virtuous Education:
William Penn's Vision for Philadelphia's Schools
(1997)

One-Armed Wonder:
Pete Gray, Wartime Baseball, and the American Dream
(McFarland, 1995)

Historic Philadelphia:
The City, Symbols & Patriots, 1681–1800
(1992)

Mike Schmidt

*Philadelphia's Hall of Fame
Third Baseman*

by
WILLIAM C. KASHATUS

McFarland & Company, Inc., Publishers
Jefferson, North Carolina, and London

Library of Congress Cataloguing-in-Publication Data

Kashatus, William C., 1959–
    Mike Schmidt : Philadelphia's Hall of Fame third baseman /
by William C. Kashatus.
        p.   cm.
    Includes bibliographical references and index.
    ISBN 0-7864-0713-1 (softcover : 55# alkaline paper) ∞
    1. Schmidt, Mike, 1949–   2. Baseball players—United
States—Biography.   3. Philadelphia Phillies (Baseball team)
I. Title.

    GV865.S36K28 2000
    796.357'092—dc21   99-48776

British Library Cataloguing-in-Publication data are available

Manufactured in the United States of America

McFarland & Company, Inc., Publishers
    Box 611, Jefferson, North Carolina 28640
    www.mcfarlandpub.com

For Peter Butler Kashatus,
who reminds me of the special bond between
a father and his son.

Acknowledgments

I began my research on this book Saturday, April 6, 1974. Mike Schmidt had just come to bat in the bottom of the ninth with the Phillies trailing the New York Mets, 4–3, in their season opener. After taking the first two pitches, Schmidt slammed a Tug McGraw fastball into the left field bleachers at Veterans Stadium. It was a two-run homer, giving the Phils a 5–4, come-from-behind victory. In that magical moment, I adopted Michael Jack as my hero. Over the years, he has provided me with twelve scrapbooks full of boxscores, several unforgettable moments and, in many ways, a moral compass by which to lead my life. For these gifts I will always be grateful to him.

This book is a fan's biography of his hero. I do not pretend to know Mike Schmidt personally. Nor was he aware that I was writing about him, until the manuscript had been completed and McFarland agreed to publish it. At that point, I felt obligated to share my work with him and ask for any correction of factual errors. He responded promptly.

Not only was he flattered that anyone would invest such time and energy on his career, but he honored my request. I'm sure that Mike disagreed with some parts of my interpretation, but he respected them, limiting his involvement to amending the facts and responding to my questions. He understood that this was my book about him, not an authorized biography. For his courtesy as well as his cooperation, I am extremely grateful.

Because I am not a Philadelphia sportswriter, a member of the Phillies organization, or a nationally recognized baseball author, it was extremely difficult to gain access to the people who influenced Schmidt's career. Therefore, I was forced to concentrate on newspaper accounts, periodicals, biographies by teammates, baseball histories, and my own insight. In the process, I found myself engaged in a constant struggle between the unconditional loyalty one feels towards a childhood hero and the necessary detachment a writer must have to undertake a serious examination of a Hall of Fame career. The complicated relationship between Schmidt and both Phillies fans and the city's sportswriters only made the challenge greater. Ultimately, I had to rely on common sense, a broader awareness of the era in which Schmidt played, and, I hope, an adequate measure of criticism as well as compassion.

Special thanks are due to Dave Kindred of *The Sporting News*, who read and commented on the manuscript; Mike Leary, who has allowed me repeated opportunities in the past to express my views on the Commentary page of *The Philadelphia Inquirer*; Sandy Shea and Frank Burgos, my current editors at *The Philadelphia Daily News*, who allow me to share my insight on Philadelphia history with their readers; and Michael O'Malley, who encouraged me to chase after that first interview with my childhood hero and then publish it in *Pennsylvania Heritage*. All of these people have helped me to become a better writer by challenging me to strike a balance between the mind and the soul.

I am also grateful to Joe Canale, AP Wide World Photos; Rick Fatica, Ohio University; Kris Hook, Corbis-Bettmann; Robert Michalski, Reading Phillies; Mark Rucker, Transcendental Graphics; Lois and Jack Schmidt, Dayton, Ohio; Dane Tilghman, who painted the image of Mike Schmidt for the cover of this book, and Brian Glasier of the Gecko Group who designed it; Milo Stewart, National Baseball Hall of Fame; and Brenda Wright, Temple University's Urban Archives, for providing photographs and images as well as the right to reproduce them.

Special thanks are also due to Zander Hollander, Associated Features, Inc., who gave permission to reprint excerpts from *Mike Schmidt: Baseball's King of Swing*.

Above all, I am indebted to my family—Mom, Dad, Jackie, Tim, and Peter, to whom this book is dedicated. Their steadfast encouragement and unconditional love have allowed me to realize my dream. I love them more than words can ever express.

Contents

Introduction

On Memorial Day 1989, my father phoned to say how sorry he was to learn that Mike Schmidt had just announced his retirement from major league baseball. He realized how much the Phillies' third baseman had meant to me, and he felt badly—for me, for Michael Jack, perhaps even for himself. In his own compassionate way, my father reassured me that one day, when I had a son of my own, the magic of baseball would return and that I'd be able to share in my boy's fantasies of his baseball hero. Although I was 28 years old, I understood that my boyhood had finally ended.

Mike Schmidt was my hero. I lived and died with him for most of his 17-year major league career. When the end came, I couldn't figure out whether I was more upset for him, for the treatment he had received from the Phillies, their fans, and the Philadelphia media, or for myself, because I would never be able to watch my childhood hero perform his magic again.

Schmidt was a Philadelphia institution. From 1973 through 1989, he led the Phils to five National League championship series and two World Series. He was selected for a dozen All-Star teams, enjoying the unique honor of being elected to his last one, in 1989, after he had retired. Voted the "Greatest Phillies Player Ever" in a poll of fans conducted in 1983, Schmidt's uniform number was ceremoniously retired by the organization seven years later, in 1990.

Schmidt was also one of baseball's premier power hitters during the 1970s and the 1980s. By the close of his celebrated career—all of which was spent in a Phillies uniform—he held or shared 14 major league records and 18 National League records. His final statistical totals place him on par with the game's greatest power hitters, immortals such as Babe Ruth, Lou Gehrig, Jimmie Foxx, and Hank Aaron. Those totals include 548 home runs (seventh best all-time in the major leagues), 1,595 RBIs (seventeenth best all-time), a .527 slugging average, and a home run ratio of one round-tripper for every 15.3 at-bats (fifth best all-time). Schmidt also led the major leagues in home runs a record eight times. Only Babe Ruth won more home run titles in one decade than the five Schmidt garnered in the 1980s. He was just as exceptional in the field, where he won ten Gold Gloves, more than any other third baseman except Brooks Robinson. Together with the Most Valuable Player Awards he won in 1980, 1981, and 1986, Schmidt's offensive and defensive production make him the best third baseman in the history of the national pastime. His election to the Baseball Hall of Fame was a foregone conclusion in 1995, his first year of eligibility. One might expect that such a superstar would be worshipped by the fans and front office alike. But Schmidt, despite his success, received fickle treatment in Philadelphia.

For years, it seemed, Schmidt just couldn't measure up. Many Philadelphia fans could not relate to his cool, withdrawn approach to the game. He was envied less for his athletic abilities than his affluence. Fathers would point to him as an example for their Little League sons during the good times and boo him during the bad. When Schmidt spoke out against the Phillies' poor trades and the incompetence of the farm system, management chastised him for not showing leadership, but was more than willing to market his image to sell their season ticket plans. Finally, after he retired, the Phillies thanked Schmidt by refusing him something he wanted and deserved: a job in the organization. It was one of the greatest affronts ever committed by a major league organization toward its franchise player.

The truth is that Philadelphia always needed Mike Schmidt. We needed him, like we need any hero, as a model for overcoming the frustrations in our lives, and as an individual onto whom we can project our fears, hopes and aggressions. That is human nature. Unfortunately, many Phillies fans failed, over the years, to appreciate the fact that Michael Jack had been a hero in every sense of the word.

Like all heroes, Schmidt demonstrated the ability to overcome adversity in his career. His rookie season, in 1973, was a nightmare. The 18 home runs and 52 RBIs he compiled that year were overshadowed by his .196 batting average and 136 strikeouts. Nevertheless, he displayed the potential to become one of the most feared power hitters in baseball. He would rebound from that rookie campaign to lead the National League in homers for the next three seasons. And while the boo-birds will never forget Schmidt's sub-par performances during the 1978 and 1988 seasons or the 1-for-20 dry spell he suffered during the 1983 World Series, the faithful fan will always remember the capacity he had for coming back.

The key to Mike Schmidt's success as a player was not his cool approach to the game but rather the pressure he placed on himself to perform. He took failure very personally. When he did display his emotions, it was as genuine as his personality—jumping on top of a pile of Phillies after the final out of the 1980 World Series or imitating a locomotive and high-stepping his way to first base after he had hit his five hundredth home run in 1987. Perseverance, dedication, and pride in performance were the keys to his success.

Ironically, few Phillies fans were ever able to understand that about Mike

Schmidt. We should have been able to view his slumps as reminders that he is only human, and then to celebrate the fact that we were fortunate enough to have a hometown hero who understood his limitations and still managed to achieve beyond the realm of the ordinary. What's most important, though, is a hero's ability to be sensitive to the needs of others. In this sense, Schmidt's efforts were grossly underestimated.

Any big name player can autograph baseballs or pose for the photographers, but what distinguishes the hero from the star is the moral code by which he lives and the example he sets for others. During the 1970s and 1980s, when other superstar athletes were doing drugs and bad-mouthing umpires, Schmidt was speaking out against drug addiction, sponsoring a host of charitable organizations, rearing a family and playing the game of baseball with all the grace and dignity one would expect of a self-proclaimed Christian athlete. He was the most responsible hero a young boy could have.

For me, a kid growing up in northeast Philadelphia, it was the 300-foot shot off the centerfield speaker on the ceiling of Houston's Astrodome and the four consecutive home runs he hit in a single game at Chicago's Wrigley Field that caught my attention. But it was the way Mike Schmidt led his life that made him my hero. Not surprisingly, by my senior year in high school, I had purposely grown a mustache, changed my uniform number to 20, and shifted from catcher to third base—a testimony of my devotion to Michael Jack. Years later when I had become a high school teacher and baseball coach, I would hear Schmidt, the parent, speak about the values he hoped to instill in his two young children—respect for authority, doing one's best at all times, leading a Christian life—the same principles by which he tried to lead his own life. It really wasn't until that moment that I realized how fortunate I was, along with an entire generation of baseball-playing adolescents, to have had a role model like Schmidt playing right here in Philadelphia.

Whether or not we choose to admit it, human beings need heroes. We try to identify ourselves with a hero to define those values that are truly important in our lives. No matter how public a hero becomes, he always remains very personal for those of us who adopt him.

Mike Schmidt will always remind me of the boyhood dream of becoming a major league baseball player, and his example continues to inspire me to strive for excellence in my personal and professional lives. And when a hero can do something like that for his fans, his career has taken him much farther than the Hall of Fame.

This book examines Schmidt's career with the Philadelphia Phillies. It is a career that dominated the most successful era in that franchise's history and one that not only coincided with but helped to influence some tremendous developments in major league baseball, including free agency and born-again Christianity. For these reasons alone, Schmidt' career demands examination. But there were other reasons I wrote the book.

Currently, Philadelphia is experiencing an all-time low in terms of pro-. fessional sports. Three of the city's four major franchises—Phillies baseball, Eagles football, and Seventy-Sixers basketball—are all struggling to become consistent winners. Even the Flyers of the National Hockey League have not been able to reproduce the Stanley Cup successes of the mid–1970s, though they have been more consistently successful than the other organizations. Regardless of the sport, however, few marquee athletes or highly rated prospects express any interest in playing here. Mike Schmidt's experience with Philadelphia's demanding fans and fickle sportswriters provides some valuable insight into the reasons for this situation.

Additionally, no one, to date, has written a serious account of Schmidt's baseball career. This is a conspicuous absence considering the subject, a Hall-of-Famer who is widely acknowledged as the greatest third baseman of all-time.

For all these reasons, a serious examination of Schmidt is long overdue. I can only hope that I have done justice to his brilliant career as well as to my own responsibility as a writer.

William C. Kashatus
Philadelphia, Pennsylvania
Summer 1999

Chapter One

The Late Bloomer

Dayton is one of southwestern Ohio's charming, small river towns. It sits on the broad flat plain at the junction of the Great Miami, Stillwater, Mad and Wolf rivers. Long a center of industry and invention, Dayton, founded in 1796, was known primarily as the home of the cash register until Orville and Wilbur Wright began experimenting with their early flying machines in 1903. Then it became "the birthplace of aviation." Acres of parks spread their forests and meadows in an emerald necklace surrounding the city limits. Just beyond are the endless ribbons of country roads. A journey down one of these serene trails reveals the breathtaking beauty of the region, with its rolling pastoral farmlands and small villages that seem untouched by the passing years. Every few miles, a baseball field can be found. They are enduring reminders that the Buckeye state was built, in part, on the big league dreams of bright-eyed youngsters. For some, the majors always remained a dream. But for others, professional baseball became a reality.

Nearly 300 natives of southwestern Ohio have made it to the major leagues. During the 1960s and 1970s, the region was a hotbed of prospective talent, and its sandlots were teeming with scouts from every professional ball-club. One of the more respected evaluators was Tony Lucadello.

Lucadello was no ordinary scout. A short, unassuming man who favored snap-brim hats, he covered the Midwest states of Ohio, Illinois and Kentucky for the Philadelphia Phillies. Like most scouts, he employed his own circle of "bird dogs," baseball aficionados who frequented the local high school and college games, informing him of any prospective talent. When he discovered a raw talent, Lucadello became almost paranoid because he didn't want to tip his hand to any of the other scouts. He hid behind bushes or watched the player from the backseat of his station wagon, going to great lengths to keep his secret. It hadn't always been that way, though.

The introduction of the amateur draft in 1965 forced Lucadello to change his approach. "In the old days," he explained, "what I would do was get in good with the prospect and his family, realizing that if my offer was close I

5

could get him to sign with me. But with the introduction of the draft, the competition for a prospect became fierce. If another scout knew my feelings about a player, he could recommend him to their front office and all my hard work would be for nothing."[1]

Mike Schmidt was one of those rare prospects Tony Lucadello coveted. In the spring of 1965, when Schmidt was still a sophomore at Fairview High School in Dayton, Lucadello received a phone call from one of his bird dogs, Ed French, who was quite impressed with the youngster. French insisted that Lucadello see Schmidt play. When Lucadello followed up on the tip, he saw that Schmidt was an "excellent athlete" and "an above average prospect." But he was still a raw talent. "Sometimes he would do things that would amaze me," recalled the idiosyncratic scout. "Other times he would make errors or just look terrible at the plate. This gave me an edge right away because other scouts would see him play and pick at all those flaws. But I sensed that Mike Schmidt was a late bloomer."[2]

Over the next two years, while Schmidt was still in high school, Lucadello watched him play a dozen times, but he never contacted the young prospect, his family or his coach for fear that another scout would find out about his interest. Instead, he watched Schmidt perform from a distance. He befriended the school's janitor, who allowed him on the roof of a building that overlooked the ball diamond. At other times, he settled in behind a tree or the opposing team's dugout.[3] While Lucadello continued to be impressed by Schmidt, other scouts dismissed the teenager as "damaged goods." Football injuries to both knees prevented him from attracting much interest from either the minor leagues or colleges. Only small Division III schools such as DePauw, Defiance, and Marietta expressed interest in him.[4] But few realized the hard work Schmidt invested in the game.

"Mike was a power hitter, who struck out a lot," said Dave Palsgrove, one of Schmidt's high school baseball coaches. "He'd hit it a mile or strike out. He had a good, strong arm and he could field. The thing you worried about was, could he hit the ball enough? There's no question though, Mike was determined. He had operations on both knees, and that held him back for a while. But he made up his mind that he wanted to excel at the game and he did." Bob Galvin, who coached Schmidt in his senior year at Fairview agreed: "Schmidt advanced a heckuva long way because he loved the game and worked hard. When I said practice was over, Mike didn't want to go home. He'd say, 'Coach, it's still too early,' and it would be dark. Or he'd say, 'Loan me some equipment and I'll get somebody to stay around and hit me pop-ups.'" According to Ron Neff, Fairview's catcher, "Mike had dedication. He'd go to the batting cages twice a week and spend one or two hours there on his own. He also learned to switch hit, being taught by Buddy Bloebaum, a scout for the California Angels. Mike just had his mind made up that he was going to play professional baseball."[5]

Since no scout expressed an interest in signing him and no college offered him an athletic scholarship, Schmidt decided to attend Ohio University and pursue a career in architecture. He was interested in drafting and knew that the school had an excellent department in architecture. Although he still intended to pursue his interest in baseball, Schmidt realized that there were more attractive players who were drawing attention from both professional ballclubs as well as Division I programs. What's more, he understood that his injured knees made him a risk for any college to recruit.

> I was about the fourth or fifth best baseball player in high school—a .250 hitter, and if you don't hit .400 in high school, nobody knows you're alive. I was always the kid with potential, but even that potential was jeopardized by a couple of major injuries in high school. I was also a late bloomer when it came to confidence and aggressiveness. I don't think I was really willing to fight for myself until I got to college. Not that I wasn't cocky in high school about my athletic ability. I knew I had as much talent for sports as anyone— I felt that whatever the season, I'd be the best athlete. But there were other players who had all the physical qualities I had and something else besides: they were meaner than I was, tougher mentally. That kind of toughness has much to do with upbringing and environment. When you come from the type of background I did—not having to fight for anything, or get out and scuffle—you grow up differently from those kids who are raised in a rougher environment. In my experience, when those two types confront each other on an athletic field, the kid with a rougher background has the upper hand. That lack of toughness, along with the injuries, curtailed whatever hopes I had of becoming a college athlete, let alone a major league baseball player. As it turned out, I went off to Ohio University with a T-square and a portfolio to study architecture, but I didn't give up on baseball.[6]

Bob Wren, the coach at Ohio University, learned of Schmidt while recruiting his teammate Ron Neff at Fairview. Although Wren didn't have any scholarship money to offer the young shortstop, he did invite him to try out for the squad. Schmidt made the team in his freshman year as a back-up to shortstop Rich McKinney. Bobcat trainer Al Hart also put him on a carefully supervised conditioning program to strengthen his knees. Schmidt was conscientious, pushing himself to redevelop his leg strength. He also abandoned his experiment with switch-hitting, discovering that he could hit only a low and inside pitch when he hit left-handed. Returning to his natural, right-handed approach, Schmidt began to crush the ball, hitting more consistently and with power.[7]

When McKinney was drafted by the Chicago White Sox in 1968, Schmidt took his place, helping OU to the first of three straight Mid-American Conference championships. The next year OU qualified for the College World Series, defeating Southern Cal, the nation's No. 1 ranked team, in the first round. The Bobcats eventually lost to Florida State and Texas to finish fourth in the tournament, but Schmidt had captured national attention with his stellar

Schmidt as a senior at Dayton's Fairview High School in 1967. Football injuries to both knees prevented him from attracting much interest from the minor leagues. When only small Division III colleges expressed an interest, he decided to attend Ohio University and pursue a career in architecture. (*Courtesy of Lois and Jack Schmidt.*)

defense and .313 average. He also earned first team NCAA All-America honors that year.

Schmidt's success came largely as the result of growing self-confidence. "It was in college that I started to gain the maturity and insight into life generally, that I needed to make it to the majors," he admitted. "I realized that teammates appreciated my ability and looked up to me, and that I had the qualities necessary to become one of the respected players of whatever team I was on—to become a leader. It looked like I might have a shot at the dream I'd once had, although I also realized I needed the right breaks and had to take advantage of them. But it did seem like I might play pro ball after all. And as I started to feel that way, I started to become a good player."[8]

In his senior year, Schmidt compiled a .330 average with 10 home runs and 45 RBIs, earning him All-America honors once again. He was also named the shortstop on The Sporting News' 1971 All-America squad and set a standing school record with 27 career home runs. Success didn't come without a lot of hard work, though.

"Mike was one of the most dedicated players I've ever had," said Wren. He worked hard to strengthen those knees and developed great upper body strength in the process. Scouts kept coming to me and asking about him, always mentioning the knees, and I pointed out that he never missed a game with us and could do anything physically required of him."[9] Two of those scouts, Lucadello and Carl Ackerman of the California Angels, paid close attention to Wren. Lucadello was so impressed with Schmidt that he insisted that Phillies' farm director Paul Owens fly out to Ohio to see Schmidt play a Saturday doubleheader against Bowling Green University. The Bobcat shortstop impressed Owens, hitting a home run, going from first to third on a routine single, and going deep in the hole at short to throw out a runner at first. Not only could Schmidt hit, run, and throw as well as some of the best prospects Owens had seen in years, but he was the kind of aggressive

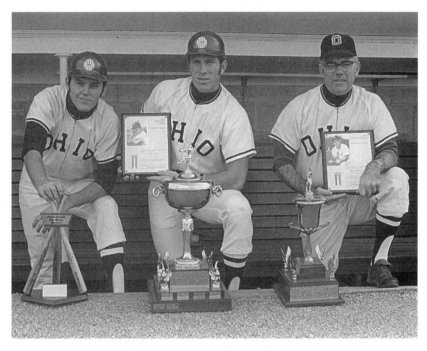

Schmidt (center) with Ohio University teammate Mike Hannah (left) and Coach Bob Wren in 1971. (*Courtesy of Ohio University.*)

player the Phillies sought. Owens immediately projected him as a third baseman.[10]

During the last few months of the 1971 college season, before the June draft, Lucadello protected his own interest in Schmidt by reminding other scouts of the shortstop's bad knees. "Mike's name would come up," admitted the Phillies scout, "and I'd say, 'Well, there's his knees, you know.' The others would nod in agreement and I could see them moving him down a notch on their lists. What they didn't know was that Mike had been on a strict weight program until his knees were as good as new."[11] At the same time, Lucadello tried to convince Owens to make Schmidt the Phillies' first pick in the draft. Unfortunately, his history of knee problems dropped Schmidt into the second round, and the Phillies selected Roy Thomas, a pitcher from California, instead. "My heart just sank," Lucadello confessed. He knew that Ackerman had Schmidt high on his list as well and thought the Phillies had lost him to the Angels. But when California made their first round selection they also chose a pitcher—Frank Tanana—and the Phillies took Schmidt in the second round.[12]

On June 11, Lucadello met with Mike and his parents at a Holiday Inn in North Dayton and signed him for $32,500 and a series of additional $2,500

At Ohio University, Schmidt success-
fully tried out for the Bobcat baseball
team. A two-time All-American at shortstop, he helped lead the squad to three
straight conference championships and
a fourth place finish in the 1970 College
World Series. (*Courtesy of Ohio University.*)

bonuses to be awarded as he advanced through the farm system
from Single A to Triple A. The next
day, Schmidt and his father flew to
Philadelphia. There he worked out
with the Phillies at Veterans Stadium, taking ground balls alongside
the organization's budding young
shortstop, Larry Bowa, and hitting
in a group that included Ron Stone,
Byron Browne, and Oscar Gamble—
fringe players on a team that was
going nowhere. Twenty-four hours
later, Schmidt made his professional
debut at Reading's Municipal Stadium against the Phillies' Class AA
Eastern League farm team.

"It just so happened that Bowa
was unable to play and the Phillies
asked me if I would want to take his
place with the big league club,"
Schmidt recalled. "John Vukovich
played third. Denny Doyle played
second. Deron Johnson was playing
first and there I was, playing shortstop." His first hit was a home run to
left field off a Mike Fremuth fast ball. It proved the margin of victory in the
Phils' 4–3 win.[13] When Schmidt crossed the plate, the Reading catcher, Bob
Boone, said, "Nice hitting, Mike." He would never forget the compliment, or
Boone's friendship as they climbed through the Phillies' farm system together.[14]

Although Schmidt's contract called for him to be sent to Peninsula, Virginia, the Phillies' Class A affiliate at the time, he remained in Reading as a
shortstop and third baseman. He hit mostly out of the eighth slot that first
season in the minors, and earned $500 a month.[15] When he finished with a
.211 average and only 8 homers and 31 RBIs in 72 games, Lucadello "caught
a little heat." But the scout stood by Schmidt, telling the Phillies' braintrust,
"This kid's a late bloomer, I've seen it before. He'll develop."[16] Part of
Schmidt's difficulty was his inability to hit breaking pitches. He admitted that
"from the time I got out of college until almost halfway through my Triple A
year, I couldn't hit breaking balls at all. They'd just freeze me at the plate."[17]
The other part of his dilemma was adjusting to life in the minor leagues.

Minor league ball is baseball in its purest form. The players haven't
become cynical, rich, or lazy yet. Their dreams allow them to tolerate the long

The Phillies' No. 2 draft pick in June 1971, Schmidt made his professional debut at Reading. In 72 games, he hit .211 with 8 HR and 31 RBI. Scout Tony Lucadello, who signed him, took some criticism for the performance but encouraged the Phillies to stay with the youngster, calling him a "late bloomer." (*Courtesy of Robert Michalski.*)

bus rides, bland food and cheap motels. All seem to arrive with raw talent and the potential for stardom. But only a few come to realize their dream of playing in the majors. Some minor leaguers become bitter, envious of another player's talent or perhaps luck. Others form a special bond, having gone through the hard times together. They come to know each other's likes and dislikes, and they learn to support each other. Schmidt was fortunate to have the support of Bob Boone during those early years of his professional career. The son of a former major league infielder, Boone was a Stanford graduate who was signed by the Phillies as a third baseman in the 1969 draft.[18] Schmidt appreciated Boone's "taking me under his wing." He was a "guy who could relate to my position, being drafted out of college. He knew I had already experienced better conditions playing college ball. He knew I was one of the 'big-deal' guys on my college team and now I was in an environment where I was starting all over, and I was away from home."[19] Schmidt and Boone would be promoted to Triple A in 1972 and then, in 1973, realize their major league dream with the Philadelphia Phillies. Others weren't as fortunate.

Schmidt's roommate, Pat Bayless, was a "can't miss" pitcher from California who rocketed through the Phillies' farm system from 1967 to 1969. From the very beginning of his professional career, there was tremendous pressure on him to succeed. In his first season, at Bakersfield, the 19-year-old Bayless went 18–8 with 217 strikeouts and a 3.04 ERA. The following season, at Reading, he went 12–8, striking out 130 and posting a brilliant 1.76 ERA. The Phillies sent him to winter ball in the Dominican Republic, and when he reported to spring training in 1969 he complained about being tired and overworked. Not surprisingly, his record at Eugene of the Class AAA Pacific Coast League dropped sharply to a disappointing 6–8 with an inflated 4.44 ERA. In 1970, Bayless was sent back to Reading, where he posted an 8–11 record with an ERA of 4.02. He realized that he had reached a crossroads. If he didn't demonstrate substantial improvement in 1971 he could kiss his dream good-bye. Bayless reported to spring training in the best condition he had ever been in. He pitched so well that he was named the winner of the Bob Carpenter Award, presented annually to the Phillies minor leaguer who "has been outstanding in attitude, hustle, desire, and advancement potential." Shortly after he received the award, however, Bayless was sent back to Reading. He was depressed and confused. Already in the middle of a painful divorce, he began taking amphetamines to ease the chronic backaches he was experiencing. Soon he was addicted to speed. The only positive thing that happened to him in those final four months of his professional career was meeting Schmidt, who would listen to Bayless' problems and go driving with him in the bright yellow Corvette he purchased with part of his signing bonus.[20]

"Whether he latched on to me or I latched on to him, I don't know," said Schmidt. "I guess he was my perception of what a pro baseball player should

The 1971 Reading Phillies were loaded with future major leaguers, including Schmidt (front row, second from left), Mike Rogodzinski (front row, third from left), Bob Boone (front row, fifth from left), and Andre Thornton (top row, third from left). Other "can't-miss" prospects such as Pat Bayless (top row, second from left) never did make it to the big leagues. (*Courtesy of Robert Michalski.*)

be like at that time. He sure looked like a good pitcher to me. We roomed together on the road. He was one of my best friends on the team at that time."[21]

One night in Pawtucket, Rhode Island, Schmidt and Bayless were sitting at a local diner having a postgame snack. Some locals looking for a fight began to harass them. Words were exchanged, and then the two players got up and left. They returned to their motel ready to call it a night when Bayless pulled out a pistol. "I had no idea he had a gun," said Schmidt. "It scared me. He also had a bag of bullets and he sat there on the bed loading this thing. He was acting as if he was going to go back there and shoot up the place, saying, 'I'm going over there to kill those guys!' I started begging him not to do it and I finally talked him out of it."[22]

Bayless was released by the Phillies that August. He returned home to California, where he grew increasingly violent, spending time in and out of mental institutions. Schmidt, on the other hand, was promoted in 1972 to the Eugene Emeralds, for whom he struggled at the plate during the early part of the season. Owens suggested that it might be in Schmidt's best interests to send him back to Reading. Manager Andy Seminick disagreed. When his average dropped to .201, Seminick decided to switch him with second baseman John Vukovich, who was also mired in a slump. It worked. Schmidt had been worrying about his hitting so much that he had jinxed himself at the plate. Having to learn a new position would take some of the pressure off. "I started playing second and it seemed like I totally concerned myself with my defense, forgetting about the pressure that was on me to hit," he said.[23]

By the end of August, Schmidt's average climbed to .291, and he had recorded 26 homers and 91 RBIs. Although he registered an eye-catching 145 strikeouts, his mental approach changed at the plate. He was more relaxed. No longer did he try to power the ball out of the park. Additionally, Schmidt's fine play at second base also bolstered the Emeralds' defense in the middle infield. A very respectable .976 fielding average (with only 8 errors) showed the Phillies that they had a fine-fielding second baseman who could fill in at shortstop or switch to third base.[24] Then things unraveled. In a game in Hawaii, Vukovich fielded a ground ball at third and flipped to Schmidt, who was covering second. When he spun around to complete the double play, his left knee locked. When the Emeralds returned to Oregon, Schmidt saw a doctor, who determined that the minor leaguer had torn the cartilage on the outside of the knee and would need surgery. While the Emeralds were competing in the Pacific Coast League playoffs, Schmidt was rehabbing the leg, preparing to go to Philadelphia for the mid–September call-up.

Shortly after the minor league playoffs, Schmidt was scheduled for surgery at Philadelphia's Temple University Hospital. At 6:00 A.M. the morning of the surgery, Dr. John R. Moore, chairman of orthopedic surgery, entered the room and looked at the knee.

"Son," he said, "I want you to follow me."

Leading the Phillies' prospect out into the hallway, Moore told him to "get in a three-point stance like a wide receiver."

Schmidt dutifully obliged.

"Now," continued Moore, "I want you to fire out and go as hard as you can down the hallway."

Groggy from medication and half-clad in a hospital gown, Schmidt got down in the three-point stance and took off, limping down the hall. The knee was so badly swollen that he could only go a few yards.

When he stopped, Moore rendered his decision: "I'm scrapping the surgery. I want you to go back and see the trainer. Rehab the knee and let me know what happens."[25]

Schmidt started on a rehab program and within a week's time was back in uniform, this time with the Philadelphia Phillies. He made his major league debut on September 12 in a game against the New York Mets at Veterans Stadium. He was inserted into the lineup in the third inning to replace third baseman Don Money. In the ninth he got his first major league hit—a single off right-hander Jim McAndrew. The following week Schmidt belted his first homer in the majors, a three-run shot off Montreal's Balor Moore that gave the Phils a 3–1 victory over the Expos. It was the only home run he hit for the Phillies in the 13 games in which he appeared for the big league club that season. His totals for the brief stint were 7 hits and 15 strikeouts in 34 plate appearances for a .206 average.[26]

Schmidt considers that season with Eugene a pivotal one in his career.

"Being on that team with players like John Vukovich, Andy Thornton, Bill Robinson, and Bob Boone—all of whom made it to the majors—made me realize how close I was to being in the big leagues," he said. "It was one of the most fun years in my entire baseball career. You're experiencing hard times with a lot of guys that you've really become close to and care about. You spend time with them. You get to know their families. They're pivotal years, and you experience it all together."[27]

But Schmidt wasn't naive. He realized that his climb to the majors was the result of a certain degree of luck. "I guess the minors were fun for me because I got the breaks and I moved right up the ladder," he admitted. "I had just enough minor league experience to say that I had a good time. If I was buried in the minors for four, five, six years, who knows what would have happened to me?"[28]

What did happen, though, was that Mike Schmidt found himself on his way to a starting third base position on a major league club that was rebuilding. He would become part of a bright future for an organization that had a rather undistinguished past.

Until the 1970s, rooting for the Philadelphia Phillies was a labor of love. No team had played as badly or lost as often as the Phillies had. With the exceptions of 1915 and 1950, when they won pennants, the Phils were better known as the perennial losers of the National League. Traditionally, Philadelphia had been an American League town, cheering on Connie Mack's more colorful—and successful—Athletics. It was difficult to compete with the nine pennants and five world championships garnered by the A's in their half century in the City of Brotherly Love, especially when your team was a halfway house to the majors for young prospects and just short of an unconditional release for fading veterans. Fortunately for Phillies owner Robert Carpenter, the Mack family ran into financial problems. Not only were the A's sold, but they were relocated to Kansas City, leading many a knowledgeable baseball fan to despair that the wrong team left Philadelphia.[29]

By 1960, the Phillies were the only baseball team in town, the unfortunate residents of a run-down stadium in a declining section of the city. But under the guidance of young manager Gene Mauch they built a talented, young team that was exciting to watch. Richie Allen and Johnny Callison provided the power. Jim Bunning and Chris Short anchored a solid pitching staff. Tony Taylor, Reuben Amaro, Bobby Wine, and Bill White composed a scrappy infield whose defense won several games for the Phils. For all their talent, though, the Phillies never achieved their potential. The closest they came was in 1964 when they made baseball infamy. They were in first place by six and a half games with twelve to play. All they needed to do was just win four of those last twelve and the Phils were a cinch to capture their third pennant. Then, for reasons that still seem inexplicable, they suffered a ten-game losing streak. When the dust cleared the Cardinals had won the pennant and the Phils finished third behind St. Louis and Cincinnati.[30]

Over the next seven years the team declined. The daily operations of the Phillies, now a club divided by racial tension, decimated by injuries, and unable to attract a successful field manager, became more than Carpenter could bear. On November 22, 1972, he handed over the ownership to his son, Ruly, who, at age 32, became the youngest president in the major leagues. But he was no stranger to the Phillies' operation.[31]

A Yale graduate who captained the baseball team, Ruly Carpenter joined the club's accounting department in 1963. The following year he and Paul Owens, a highly respected scout in the organization, began evaluating the talent in the Phillies' low minors. In 1965 when Owens was named farm director, Ruly became his assistant. Then, in 1972, both men became the brain trust for the organization, Carpenter as owner and Owens in the dual role as general manager and field manager.[32] The Phillies also moved into the brand new, multisport Veterans Stadium in South Philadelphia, giving the team and its fans a spirited boost. No longer would they have to play before dwindling crowds in the dilapidated, old Connie Mack Stadium in North Philadelphia. "There were still serious problems with the team though," Owens admitted. "I felt I knew what we had in the way of talent in the minors. Since I've always considered myself a good evaluator I figured if I lived, ate and slept with the players on the parent club, I would know just what I had and I had confidence that I could turn the thing around."[33]

What Owens had inherited was a horrible ballclub. The 1972 Phillies posted a 59–97 record, finishing sixth in the National League's Eastern Division, 37½ games out of first place. Pitcher Steve Carlton, who went 27–10 that season, was responsible for 46 percent of the team's victories. Aside from Carlton, the only bright spots on the team were Larry Bowa, a fine defensive shortstop; center fielder Willie Montañez, a self-confessed hotdog whose flamboyant fielding and power-hitting endeared him to the fans; and Greg Luzinski, a solid prospect who hit .281 with 18 homers and 68 RBIs that season. The strength of the organization, however, could be found in the minor leagues, where prospects such as Schmidt, catcher Bob Boone, and pitchers Larry Christenson and Dick Ruthven were refining their raw talent.[34]

In 1973, Owens entrusted the Phillies to Danny Ozark and moved back upstairs to the front office. Ozark had played and managed in the Dodger organization for more than 20 years, more recently for Walter Alston as third base coach in Los Angeles. He was considered the odds-on favorite to succeed Alston when the Dodger manager retired. When he arrived at the Phillies' spring training complex in Clearwater, Florida, Ozark made it clear that he would emphasize the fundamentals. It was a decision that would prove to be beneficial to a very young team sorely lacking in the basics.[35]

At the same time, Owens began making personnel changes. Realizing that the Phillies needed starting pitching and believing that Schmidt had the potential to be the club's third baseman of the future, the general manager traded Don Money to the Milwaukee Brewers for Jim Lonborg and Ken Brett. Money, who had been acquired from Pittsburgh in 1968, was the Phillies' regular third baseman from 1970 on. Although he hit .295 with 14 homers and 66 RBIs that year, he became expendable after failing to hit higher than .223 the next two seasons.[36] Lonborg, on the other hand, had won the Cy Young Award with Boston in 1967, helping the Red Sox to an American League pennant. Although his career had been sidetracked by injuries, Owens believed that the tall right-hander still had the potential to be a consistent winner.[37] Brett was a solid prospect who was worth a risk. Owens also needed a first baseman, so he moved center fielder Willie Montañez there and traded outfielders Oscar Gamble and Roger Freed to the Cleveland Indians for Del Unser, a fine defensive center fielder who had displayed promise as a line-drive hitter earlier in his career. Bob Boone became the Phillies' regular catcher and Schmidt split time at third base with a journeyman veteran infielder, César Tovar.[38]

Under Ozark's leadership, the Phillies showed clear signs of improvement in 1973. The pitching was solid. Lonborg, Brett, and rookie Wayne Twitchell each won 13 games. Had Carlton not slipped to 13–20, the Phils might have been in contention for a division title. Most of the power was supplied by Luzinski (.285 avg., 29 HR, 97 RBI) and Bill Robinson (.288 avg., 25 HR, 65 RBI), a retread outfielder who buckled under the mantle of high expectations with the Yankees but was quickly finding his batting stroke in Philadelphia. Schmidt contributed 18 home runs and 52 RBIs in his rookie season, but club officials were extremely concerned about his high strikeout ratio—136 in 367 at-bats.[39]

At least once every homestand, Ozark would meet with Owens and new farm director Dallas Green to discuss the 23-year-old rookie. Owens and Green wanted to send him back to the minors, believing that he was over-matched at the plate. Ozark convinced them to keep Schmidt put. The Phillies were a last-place team whose future rested with a young power hitter like Schmidt. Why not let him play and learn? "Mike had proven he could hit Triple A pitching, what was he going to prove down there?" reasoned Ozark. "I said to Owens, we might as well let him play. He had great hands, quick reactions, and his swing was like a Ben Hogan golf swing. The ball came off the bat like a rocket. He didn't muscle the ball. It was all timing and bat speed. He had so much talent, it was only a matter of time before he put it all together."[40] At the same time, Ozark assumed a paternalistic attitude toward Schmidt. He began calling his rookie third baseman "Dutch," a term of endearment for players of German ancestry. He summoned Schmidt to his office on almost a daily basis to give him advice. Against some of the tougher right-handers, Ozark would bench him, particularly when Schmidt was in a slump.[41] While Ozark's intentions were good, his approach was clumsy at best. Schmidt resented being called "Dutch," as if he were a "big, dumb kid." He interpreted

Ozark's treatment of him as critical. "Danny never taught me much as a player," Schmidt said years later reflecting on his rookie season. "He thought I was a stubborn kid. He treated me more like my father, disciplining me, yelling at me, using me as an example."[42]

Schmidt was also going through the hazing process all rookies experienced in those days. Montañez, who had suffered the same ridicule two seasons earlier, was merciless in his treatment of the rookie third baseman. Whenever Schmidt walked past him in the batting cage, Montañez would pretend to sneeze as though he had caught a cold from Schmidt's swings and the draft they created—an unpleasant reminder of his high strikeout ratio.[43] Bowa, who had a chip on his shoulder from the day he heard that the Phillies signed Schmidt, a college All-America shortstop, also rode him endlessly. Bowa felt that he had already paid his dues, scratching and clawing his way up through the Phillies' farm system. A fiery, intense competitor who had to work hard at the game, Bowa felt threatened by Schmidt's abilities. The more threatened he felt, the more he antagonized his younger teammate.[44]

Between Ozark's paternalism, his teammates' hazing, and the incessant booing of the hometown fans, Schmidt became depressed. The more he struggled at the plate, the more frustrated and bewildered he became. "All I wanted to do my first season," he said, "was hit the ball out of sight. I got into trouble by pulling away from the plate instead of simply swinging the bat to make contact."[45] Schmidt tried to forget about his problems by partying every night. He'd get lost in the nightlife of Philadelphia's dance clubs. "If I do good, I celebrate by partying," he admitted. "If I do badly, I forget it by partying. I'm young, I can handle it."[46] In fact, he couldn't. The partying drained him. He would sleep through the next day until it was time to go to the ballpark. Sometimes he would rise early enough to play golf at the city's suburban courses with Steve Carlton, who had a special way of encouraging a positive approach to the game among the younger Phillies players. It was after one of those golf outings that Schmidt met Donna Wightman, a waitress at Valley Forge Stouffers.

Schmidt walked into the restaurant with Carlton after a September morning golf game. Donna recognized the Phillies' pitcher from his MAB paint commercial on television but didn't know his friend since she didn't have any real interest in baseball. Trained as a commercial artist who also toured the country as a warm-up singer for the rock band the Byrds, Wightman was working part-time as a cocktail waitress at Valley Forge Stouffers. Schmidt immediately took a liking to her and mustered the courage to ask for her "autograph." "It was the only line he ever fed me," Donna would muse years later. "I thought: 'Hah, who is this guy?'" They began dating that September and were married the following February. She was 21 years old. He was 24.[47] The marriage provided the kind of stability Schmidt needed in his life. No longer would he spend his nights partying, but would return home after the ball game. Donna was a good listener who gave her husband a better perspective, helping him to understand that there was more to life than baseball.

At the same time, Schmidt began to develop more confidence in his ability to play the game. After the 1973 campaign ended, Ozark spent two weeks with his third baseman in the Veterans Stadium batting cage trying to figure out why a player with as much power and potential as Schmidt made it so hard on himself at the plate. Schmidt was not very enthusiastic about the idea, but he agreed to it.

"At first, I think Mike resented my postseason instruction," said Ozark, "but he got over it when he realized the practice was for his own benefit. Nor was there anything drastic about the change I suggested in his hitting. It was just a slight change in the way he held the bat and his stance. The ability was there. It was just a matter of improving his concentration. You know he hasn't had much experience and it was a big step for him taking over the third base job on a big league club. But with that rookie year behind him, I think Mike has a great future. He can field and he's become one of the best base stealers on the club."[48]

Schmidt also played winter ball in Caguas, Puerto Rico, in the off-season. It was an impressive team whose roster included Gary Carter, Larry Christenson, and Jim Essian. Bobby Wine, former Phillies shortstop who served as a coach for Ozark, managed the team. He was much more soft-spoken than Ozark and gave Schmidt the distance he needed to emerge on his own. Occasionally, Wine would offer an insightful remark: "You sting the ball when you hit it, Mike. But you also strike out too often. Remember, when you're up with a man in scoring position, you don't have to drive the ball 700 feet. Just hit it to right center or left center. You're a good player, a good hitter."[49] It was exactly the kind of encouragement Schmidt needed to hear.

When Caguas advanced to the Latin American World Series, Schmidt put Wine's advice to work. In a game against Hermosilla, Mexico, he adopted a more relaxed approach at the plate. He began driving the ball even farther than he had during the 1973 season. "All these years," he told Wine, "I thought you had to swing hard to hit it far. But trying to hit that way created all of my problems. Now I realize that you can swing easy and get the same results."[50]

Schmidt developed a killer instinct that winter. He didn't take as many pitches as he had during his rookie season, and he became a lot more aggressive and self-assured at the plate. The success carried over into the 1974 season. The Phillies' "late bloomer" was ready to bloom.

Chapter Two

An Honorary Brother

Mike Schmidt emerged as the Phillies' quintessential power hitter in the mid–1970s. He won three straight National League home run titles with 36 in 1974, 38 in 1975, and another 38 in 1976. He also drove in 95 or more RBIs in each of those seasons. While Schmidt continued to struggle with his strike-out ratio, averaging 155 Ks a season over that same period, he also raised his batting average to a very respectable .264. Together with his excellent defense at third base, Schmidt's hitting earned him the respect of the fans, who voted him onto the 1974 All-Star squad by write-in ballot! With Schmidt's star rising, the Phillies won the National League East for three straight years, beginning in 1976.

Schmidt's development was doubtless aided by a support system of African-American players who offset the criticism he was taking from other teammates. Dave Cash, Bill Robinson, Dick Allen, and Garry Maddox encouraged him, showing him how to channel his frustrations in ways that enhanced his performance and helped the ballclub. Schmidt reciprocated. He befriended the black players, confiding in them, crediting them for his success whenever he felt it was their due. His was a refreshing example for the white players who performed for a franchise haunted by an inglorious history of race relations.

The Philadelphia Phillies had always been a racially segregated team in a racially segregated city. During Jackie Robinson's quest to break the color barrier in 1947, the Phillies' brass actually phoned Brooklyn Dodgers' president Branch Rickey before the two teams met and told him "not to bring that nigger here." Predictably, the Phillies treated Robinson worse than any other team in the National League whenever he appeared in Philadelphia. Pitchers threw at his head, infielders purposely spiked him on the base paths, and—in one of the lowest moments in baseball history—the team humiliated Robinson by standing on the steps of their dugout, pointing their bats at him and making gun shot sounds.[1]

The Phillies were the last team in the National League to integrate. They did not field a black player until 1957 when John Kennedy appeared in five games for the Phils at third base—a full decade after Robinson broke the color line. Even then, the Phillies maintained segregated spring training facilities, a practice that was finally abandoned in 1962. In wasn't until the mid–1960s, with the arrival of players like Johnny Briggs, Bill White, and the team's first African-American superstar Dick Allen, that the team regularly fielded black players.[2] In fact, Allen forced Philadelphia baseball and its fans to come to terms with the racism that existed in the city in the 1960s and 1970s. He did not have the self-discipline or tact of Jackie Robinson, but Allen did serve the same purpose for Philadelphia baseball while also exemplifying the growing black consciousness in the national pastime itself. While his unexcused absences, candid opinions, and pregame beer drinking earned him some of the harshest press in Philadelphia's sport history, his tape-measure home runs and exceptional speed gained for him the tremendous admiration of fellow players—both black and white.

Dick Allen never had it easy in Philadelphia and it wasn't entirely his own fault. In 1963 the Phillies sent their 21-year-old outfield prospect to their minor league affiliate in Little Rock, making him the first black ballplayer in Arkansas history. That season was a nightmare for him. He received threatening phone calls, had the windshield of his car painted with "nigger, go home" signs, and could not be served in a restaurant unless accompanied by a white player. Still, Allen managed to do more than survive.

The Phillies called him up in September, and he proceeded to hit major league pitching at a .292 clip. The next season, Allen had to deal with the pressure of a summer-long pennant race while playing third base, a new position. While most Phillies fans remember 1964 for the team's infamous collapse in the final two weeks of the season, some may recall that Allen's .318 average, 29 homers and 91 RBIs kept the team in the pennant race for most of the season—a performance that earned for him the National League's Rookie of the Year Award.

Despite the fact that Allen hit .300 and averaged 30 homers and 90 RBIs for the next five years in Philadelphia, the fans never forgave him for a 1965 altercation with a popular white veteran player, Frank Thomas, who was subsequently traded. They booed him every night, threw pennies, bolts, or beer bottles at him whenever he played the outfield, and sent him hate mail. The press often treated him less sympathetically than white ballplayers who were just as outspoken. Finally, in 1969, Allen was traded to the St. Louis Cardinals. He had been a victim of the Phillies' racism.[3]

Although Philadelphians live in a sports culture where history seems to be measured in minutes—not years—and forgetfulness is common, the city's blacks still hadn't forgiven the Phillies for their treatment of Robinson or Allen. Those ugly memories lingered into the 1970s, along with the feelings of many African-American baseball fans that the Phillies were a racist organization in a segregated city.

Dick Allen was known as "Richie" when he won Rookie of the Year honors in 1964. For the next five seasons, he hit .300 and averaged 30 home runs and 90 RBIs. After a five-year hiatus with the Cardinals, Dodgers and White Sox, the enigmatic slugger returned to Philadelphia, where he befriended Mike Schmidt. (*Courtesy of Transcendental Graphics.*)

During the 1970s, Philadelphia was experiencing middle class "white flight" to the suburbs. Whites were escaping the crime, drugs and gang warfare of North and West Philadelphia where the black population had relocated from the old-time ghettos. While whites made their new homes in the outlying suburbs of Merion, Abington, Haverford, Malvern, Swarthmore, and Bucks County, the hope of the future for the city lay with upwardly mobile black families whose wage earners were employed in banks, insurance companies, law offices and government agencies and lived in sections of the city like Germantown, Mount Airy, Queen Village, and Fairmount.[4] But it was still a struggle for them.

Frank Rizzo, a maverick Democrat and former police commissioner, was mayor. His streetwise, shoot-from-the-hip, tough cop style became synonymous with the public's image of Philadelphia—and it wasn't good. He viewed city government as an institution for preserving law and order and only secondarily as an instrument to provide social services. Consequently, very little was done to improve the quality of life in the city, resulting in less civility and more physical self-expression. He also antagonized the black community with his outspoken comments on race, voicing sentiments previously unthinkable among responsible public officials and couched in rhetoric of physical intimidation. His charisma and personality inspired unreasoned loyalty on one side and fear, as well as violent opposition, on the other. The loyalty withstood scandals, increased taxes, lie-detector tests and national derision.

The fear led his opponents to use lawsuits, the press and intraparty warfare to loosen his control of the city.[5]

In fact, the Phillies, who were trying to distance themselves from a controversial past, might have been one of the few rays of hope for a city struggling with the issue of race relations. The team added a significant number of black players to its roster in the 1970s. Among them were Bill Robinson and Dave Cash. Robinson, an outfielder, was once touted by the Yankees as the "next Mickey Mantle." But he buckled under all the publicity and pressure, becoming a well-traveled veteran. The Phillies salvaged his career from the Pacific Coast League in 1972, and the following season he began to hit major league pitching like the experts had predicted years before.[6] Robinson helped Schmidt adjust to the high expectations that the front office had for him by offering encouraging comments and, when necessary, advice on how to deal with the pressure. Cash was even more influential.

A scrappy veteran second baseman with Pittsburgh, Cash, at the young age of 26, knew what it was like to win. Signed by the Pirates in 1969, he took over second base from Bill Mazeroski two years later and became an instrumental player on a team that captured three division titles and a world championship. His experience, enthusiasm, and aggressive play were just what the young Phillies needed. Owens realized the need for veteran leadership and traded pitcher Ken Brett to Pittsburgh for Cash. The new second baseman made an immediate impact, providing a steadying influence in the infield and giving the team the confidence they needed to win. Cash coined the slogan "Yes We Can!" as a rallying cry for the young team that came to believe they could win.[7] His effect on Schmidt was especially noticeable.

"When I came to the Phillies in 1974, Mike had all the tools but he didn't have the confidence," recalled Cash. "He was constantly doubting himself. And the fans rode him pretty hard. I spent a lot of time with him, trying to get him to block out the crowd."[8] It worked. Cash's constant encouragement restored Schmidt's confidence, providing the inspiration for a sensational season in 1974.

On opening day at Veterans Stadium against the New York Mets, the Phillies found themselves trailing 4–3 in the ninth with one out and a runner on first base. Schmidt came to bat facing reliever Tug McGraw and homered to left field to win the game, 5–4.[9] That at-bat seemed to set the tone for Schmidt's entire season. By July he had already collected 18 homers and 56 RBIs and was crushing the ball, hitting at a .319 clip. Perhaps the most impressive display of his power, however, came in a June tenth at-bat in Houston's Astrodome. It came in the first inning. Cash, the lead-off hitter, walked. Bowa followed with a single. Schmidt, hitting out of the third slot, jumped on a Claude Osteen fast ball, hitting it so high and so hard that the Astros' center fielder, César Cedeño, retreated to the wall just to see how far it would sail. But after soaring 340 feet in the air, the ball crashed into a public-address speaker 110 feet above straightaway center field. It dropped straight down, landing about 325 feet from the plate. Had the speaker not been there, the Astrodome's engineers estimated that Schmidt's home run might have traveled anywhere from 500 to 600 feet. Instead, he had a ground-rule single, since the speaker, as a fixed object, is in fair territory. Just to prevent a repeat occurrence, the Astros raised the speaker to 173 feet after the game, a 12–0 Phillies victory.[10]

"I knew the ball was going out," admitted Cedeño after the game, "but I continued running because I wanted to see how far it would go. I know one thing, it was over everything. I never saw a ball hit so hard in my life. I've seen some real line shots by Richie Allen and guys like that, but nothing like this."[11] Schmidt was just as amazed. "I knew it was a good hit," he said, "but the ball doesn't carry well in the Astrodome so I didn't know how far it was going. Running to first base, I realized it hit something up there. I didn't know what, but something. It all happened so fast, I really wasn't sure of the ground rule. What can pop into your mind at a time like that? But after the umpire held me at first base, I realized the ball had hit the speaker and that it cost me a home run. I'd like to have seen it go all the way, just to see how far it would've gone."[12]

The "homer that wasn't" captured national attention for Schmidt, provoking a write-in campaign to get the 24-year-old third baseman elected to the National League's All-Star squad. Because he had such a dismal rookie season, Schmidt's name didn't appear on the ballot. But with the aid of the write-in campaign, which was conducted by Howard Eskin, a young intern at a Philadelphia radio station, and the Phillies, who hired a helicopter to airlift 100,000 votes to All-Star headquarters to beat the election deadline, Schmidt finished second to the Dodgers' Ron Cey. National League manager Yogi Berra of the Mets eventually picked the power-hitting third baseman for the squad, adding, "The guy is having a fantastic year. And besides, I don't want to get shot next time I go to Philly."[13]

Schmidt joined Carlton, Bowa, and Cash as the Phillies' representatives at the All-Star game, which was played in San Diego that year. He went to bat twice and walked both times. More importantly, his election to the team gave him confidence that he could compete with the very best in the major leagues. Schmidt finished the 1974 campaign with a league-leading 36 homers, 116 RBIs and a .282 average, 86 points higher than that of his rookie season. Other Phillies demonstrated significant improvement as well.

Cash was just as impressive on the field as he was in the clubhouse, leading the National League in at-bats with 687 and hitting .300. His example inspired Bowa, who raised his batting average to .275—64 points higher than his average of the previous season. Montañez returned to the .300 mark. Boone proved more than adequate behind the plate and handled a respectable pitching staff with the savvy of a seasoned veteran. The pitching improved

All-Star infielders of the 1974 Phillies: Dave Cash (left) and Larry Bowa (center) join Schmidt for the mid-summer classic played that year at Pittsburgh's Three Rivers Stadium. (*Courtesy of UPI/Corbis-Bettmann*.)

as well. Lonborg led the staff in victories with 17, Carlton chalked up 16 wins, Ron Schueler, who joined the Phils from Atlanta, added another 11 victories, and Dick Ruthven contributed an additional nine. With those kinds of numbers, the Phillies led their division through the spring and much of the summer only to fall behind Pittsburgh in late August. Still, they finished the season in third place, only 8 games out. It was the first time the team finished out of the cellar since 1971, and the first time they finished higher than fifth place since 1969, when the National League was reorganized into eastern and western divisions.[14]

When asked to explain his change in fortune from a dismal rookie year, Schmidt replied, "I guess I just learned to relax. Last year I was in and out of the lineup and when I was in I probably tried too hard to do well because I was wondering if I'd be in the next day. I wanted to relax last season, but I couldn't. I was as tight as a drum. This year, when I go to the plate, I'd say 70 to 80 percent of the time, I'm at ease just looking to hit the ball hard somewhere. When you come up to the plate that way, your natural instincts take over."[15]

Schmidt also acknowledged the tremendous impact Robinson and Cash had on his own attitude. "Before those guys came to the Phillies it wasn't too much fun to come to the ballpark," he admitted. "Robbie had a lot to do with the early success in my career. He was one of the first guys who gave me a lot of confidence by telling me that I was a good player and that I was going to be successful some day. Dave Cash also helped me in terms of having a good, positive attitude around the clubhouse. He always seemed to say the right things to me. That was a big difference from guys like Bowa, Luzinski, and Montañez, who were ragging on me all the time, kidding me about striking out. There was a bit of jealousy there and I saw it as mean-spirited, no question. I found a solace from the black players who, for some reason, took a liking to me. There was just a sensitivity there that I felt very comfortable with."[16]

The resentment towards Schmidt was understandable. Montañez was 26 years old, Luzinski was only 23, and Schmidt was 24. All were about the same age. All had tremendous offensive potential but had only begun to tap into it. Montañez enjoyed an outstanding 1971 season as he hit 30 home runs and drove in 99, earning a second-place finish in the balloting for Rookie of the Year. His flamboyant play in the field and the almost casual manner in which he walked up to the plate, flipping the bat in one hand from handle to barrel, made him popular with the fans who dubbed him "Willie the Phillie." By 1974, however, the center fielder's home run total had slipped to 7, and Schmidt's success only added to the pressure Montañez felt to produce.[17]

Luzinski, the Phillies' top pick in the 1968 June free agent draft, also enjoyed an impressive rookie season in 1972, collecting 18 home runs, 68 RBIs, and a .281 average. The following season he established himself as one of the top young power hitters in the game by clouting 29 homers, driving in 97 runs and compiling a .285 average. Big things were predicted for the "Bull" in 1974. He was being compared to Dick Allen, Willie Stargell, and Johnny Bench, some of the premier power hitters in the game. Standing 6' 1" and weighing 225 pounds, he was built like a defensive lineman, leading the prognosticators to believe that a 50 homer season was well within his reach. But Luzinski battled a weight problem, and in 1974 that problem landed him on the disabled list for most of the season when he tore a ligament in his right knee.[18] Schmidt's bat filled the offensive void left by Luzinski that season. The young third bagger's 36 homers, 116 RBIs and .282 average were in fact better than the numbers the Bull had produced in the past, and Luzinski knew it.

Bowa was a different story. He worked hard, toiling in the Phillies' farm system for four years before making it to the majors in 1970. When he finally made it, Bowa didn't even hit his weight, but then-manager Frank Lucchesi stayed with him at shortstop. Lucchesi had a fierce allegiance to Bowa because they had come up together, as player and coach, in the farm system. But Lucchesi's tenure as manager would be short-lived. When the Phillies made Schmidt their second selection in the June draft, they had planned to make him their future shortstop. Word got back to Bowa. "Right away, I've got a chip on my shoulder," he admitted years later. When they flew Schmidt to Philadelphia to work out with the big league club, Bowa was seething with anger. "I said, 'Screw this guy, Mike Schmidt.' Who does he think he is, some big deal? He's a college kid. Everything's cool with him. He takes ground balls with me at the Vet and after he worked out they sent him to Reading—double A—and he tore it up. I remember a comment he made, something like, 'I plan on playing shortstop in Philadelphia.' And my reply was, 'Not as long as I'm here!' So I kept working and the more I read about Mike Schmidt, the harder I worked. You know the rest of it … he ended up playing third base!"[19]

Predictably, Schmidt viewed Bowa as a hard-nosed competitor who tended to place individual success above team success in their early years together.

> Larry was always quick to criticize other people's work habits. There's an average type of worker, a guy with poor habits, and there's the hard worker. And the hard-working people, the people who are consumed by their profession, always seem to feel they should get more out of it because they put more into it. Sometimes a guy comes along who gets a lot more out of it than he puts into it. I probably put a hell of a lot more work into playing the game later in my career than I did in my first four or five years. All of a sudden, I started setting standards as a player that I eventually understood couldn't be kept up without hard work. Still, I don't think I've ever had the kind of work habits that Bowa had. He worked endlessly, trying to make himself into a better hitter and, to his credit, he became a .300 hitter. He got the most of his talent. I don't have to tell you that. He got the maximum out of the talent he had. As a young player, he came to an organization that was really hurting. He was forced into the big leagues and had to learn to play and to win at the big league level. Whatever he lacked in ability he made up for in desire and hard work.
>
> Over time, Bowa made himself a great shortstop. We jelled. We were as good a left side of the infield as there was at the time. But he never did anything real fluidly. He just caught everything that came his way and got it to first base. It never looked real fluid or pretty or graceful, but he always got the job done.[20]

To be sure, Schmidt and Bowa were players with two very different personalities. Bowa was fiery, aggressive and competitive to the point of being ruthless at times. He had to work for everything he got in terms of his fielding and hitting. Even then, his style wasn't too pretty. He simply got the job done, both offensively and defensively. Schmidt, on the other hand, was a gifted athlete who made the hard plays look easy, almost graceful. He spent only two years in the minor leagues and, though he struggled with his hitting, his bat was always very capable of spelling the margin of victory in a game. Although Schmidt was every bit as intense as Bowa, he tended to internalize those feelings. That's what bothered Bowa the most about him. "I knew that it was killing him inside when he was in a slump," said the fiery, little infielder. "I'd ask him, 'Why don't you show some emotion? Hit something. Go mad. Go berserk!'" [21] Schmidt didn't appreciate the advice.

"Larry was a great clubhouse needler, but he didn't have great timing," said Schmidt. "There were times when he didn't needle people and I think he should have. There were times when he needled me that I thought it would be best to lay off. One time, I got so angry in a clubhouse in Houston that I almost wanted to kill him. I probably would have if there weren't four other players there to separate us."[22]

Bowa admits that he probably set new standards when it came to riding teammates: "Oh yeah, I did a good job. I'd get on players. But I'd know who to get on. I got on Luzinski a lot more than I ever got on Schmidt. But Greg knew me. We were close friends. He also took a lot of crap from the fans and, in my opinion, not deservedly so. I thought that he was a much better clutch hitter than Schmidt in those early years. Back then, Bull would come up when we were behind and hit one out. Schmitty would always hit his homers when the score was 7–1, 7–2."[23]

Schmidt and Bowa only gave each other respect begrudgingly during their early years together. Over the next six years, however, both players matured, proving worthy of the other's respect. Winning had a way of mending their personal conflict, and the Phillies would become perennial winners.

In 1975, Owens made two more transactions in his quest to capture a pennant. He acquired the rights to Dick Allen's contract from the Atlanta Braves, and, to make room for the All-Star first baseman, he traded Montañez to the San Francisco Giants for center fielder Garry Maddox. Those two acquisitions not only doubled the number of blacks on the club, but also added to Schmidt's support system. In fact, Schmidt, who "idolized Allen" during his days "playing American Legion ball back in Ohio," was instrumental in getting the slugger back into a Phillies uniform.[24]

Allen had a controversial career since leaving Philadelphia in 1969. He spent single seasons with the St. Louis Cardinals and Los Angeles Dodgers, teams he believed he could help. But his enigmatic personality divided the clubhouse. Both organizations gave up on him and traded him off for considerably less talent than he was worth. He landed with the Chicago White Sox in 1972 and put up numbers that earned him the American League MVP that year. Perhaps the change to a new league was the answer. Allen enjoyed three very productive seasons in Chicago before retiring in September of 1974. He returned to his farm in Perkasie, Pennsylvania, intending to pursue his "other" passion—raising thoroughbred horses. But the Phillies believed that Allen still had a lot of baseball left in him. The .302 average and 32 homers he compiled in 1974 certainly seemed to reinforce that feeling. The following April, a small contingent of Phillies—Schmidt, Cash and broadcaster Rich Ashburn—paid the recently retired slugger a visit.

"It was a conversation I wouldn't forget," said Allen. "Schmidt was talking about the Phils needing some additional clout, a big stick in the lineup to go with his and Luzinski's. He said something about 'Schmidt-Luzinski-Allen firepower.' Cash was rapping about the brothers on the Phils' team and how they could use a veteran to inspire them. And ol' Richie Ashburn was telling tales about how much the city of Philadelphia had changed for the better. That was as specific as it got, but I got the message: 'Come home Dick. We love you. They're gonna love you!'

"At first I figured it had to be a joke. It's not my style to return to the scene of the crime. But I had to admit the idea of coming home did fire me up a bit. I always did like surprises—even when the surprises were on me. When they left the farm that day, I hugged them all. I was touched to feel wanted by guys who played for the Phillies."[25]

That visit was followed by another. This one from Ashburn and Hall of Famer Robin Roberts. Again, the Phillies attempted to reconcile with their one-time Rookie of the Year. "No specific requests were made and no promises given," insists Allen.[26] A few days later, the *Philadelphia Inquirer* reported that Commissioner Bowie Kuhn was investigating the Phillies for tampering with the retired slugger. Almost immediately, the White Sox sold Allen to the Atlanta Braves. Of course, Allen had no intention of playing for Atlanta, not after the painful experience of playing in the South at the start of his career. The Braves quickly realized that fact and, after Kuhn dismissed the tampering charges, dealt him to the Phillies.[27]

Allen's decision to return to the Phillies shocked the baseball world. To those who really knew him, though, it was consistent with his approach to the game itself. Allen's career had always been distinguished by predictable unpredictability. But two things were certain: Allen was blessed with the exceptional talent of a superstar and, at the age of 33, he still had not realized his full potential. He knew it, too. Allen understood that he had not fulfilled anybody's expectations—the fans, the baseball world's or, sadly, his own. In 11 previous seasons, he hit 40 home runs once, drove in 100 runs three times, and never had the experience of being on a pennant winner. Only twice did he match the offensive productivity of his 1964 Rookie of the Year season—in 1966, when he belted 40 homers, and in 1972, when he batted .308, hit 37 home runs and drove in 113 RBIs to win the American League's MVP Award. Instead, his career was troubled by an odd assortment of injuries and an inability to cope with people who had difficulty understanding him.[28] Perhaps a second chance in Philadelphia is what he needed. And he got it.

Ashburn was correct. Phillies baseball had changed in the six years since Allen had last played for the team. There was no more Connie Mack Stadium. Instead, the Phillies played in brand new Veterans Stadium. The crowds were suburban and white. There was a new owner in Ruly Carpenter, who seemed more compassionate, more approachable than his father had in the 1960s.

Conditions seemed right both for a reconciliation and, with a little luck, for that pennant that Allen desired. He was excited to return to his old team, which, as he put it, "finally entered the twentieth century in terms of race." In the 1960s, Allen believed that he represented "a threat to white people in Philadelphia." "I wore my hair in an Afro," he recalled. "I said what was on my mind. I didn't take shit. But now Philadelphia and its fans seemed to have changed. The brothers on the team represented a new generation of black ball players. They were talented and proud of it and didn't take a back seat to anybody. In terms of pure baseball, I looked around that clubhouse and liked what I saw. We had Schmitty at third base and there's no telling what he could do, Cash at second, Bowa at short, Bob Boone behind the plate, me at first. Pretty tough infield. We had Luzinski and Maddox in the outfield, and platooners Ollie Brown and Mike Anderson to round it out. We had pitchers like Steve Carlton and Jim Lonborg, and Tug McGraw in the bullpen. I remember thinking that maybe with this bunch I could get myself a World Series ring after all."[29]

Allen returned to the Phillies' lineup against the Cincinnati Reds in mid-May. It was a hero's homecoming. His new teammates openly embraced him. The energy level on the club seemed to soar. The fans were even more receptive, even patronizing. If Allen made a miscue during those first few games back—as he did several times, having missed all of spring training—it was excused. He was cheered constantly for routine plays. Perhaps the most paternalistic expression of fan appreciation came in a game against San Francisco. After struggling all evening against Giant pitching, Allen, in the tenth inning, hit a sharp liner that was misplayed by the third baseman. When the winning run scored on the error, the Phillies' "faithful" erupted with applause and demanded a curtain call from their new hero.[30] Even the press was friendly.

Allen found himself glibly answering the questions of sportswriters he had refused to talk to six years earlier. Now following the fans' lead, they were a band of admirers toting pads and pens, hanging on to his every word. Six years before, the press had run Allen out of town, steadfastly calling him "Richie," knowing fully that he found the name denigrating because it sounded like a boy's name. He had requested time and again that he be referred to as "Dick Allen." Now they graciously deferred to his request.[31] While all the media hype unfolded, Ruly Carpenter, who understood the fickle nature of the local press, stood watching, hoping the press wouldn't run his new slugger out of town again. "I hope to hell they leave him alone," he said quietly. "I could never understand why they got on him so when he was here before. He's a serious, dedicated athlete, he's a great team player, and really, he never did anything you could consider bad for the game of baseball. Hell, Babe Ruth was drunk all the time, whored around like mad, set a lousy example for kids, and there was never a bad word written about him. Allen would show up late for a practice once and they'd crucify him. How do you explain it?"[32] Carpenter was missing the point: You don't explain it. Not in Philadelphia, where exceptions are the rule, especially when it comes to the Phillies. The fans, the press and the culture itself are fickle. That is why Allen, for all of his unpredictability, was a soul mate for Mike Schmidt.

Like Allen, Schmidt, in 1975, had superstar potential and an extremely sensitive ego. Both men were natural athletes in the truest sense of the term. Both were blessed with tall, muscular, athletic builds. Both were power hitters with high strikeout ratios. And both had to labor under the unrealistic expectations of the Philadelphia fans and the local media. The same was said about Allen as was said about Schmidt in 1975: "The only thing that can keep Mike Schmidt from being a superstar is Mike Schmidt. He has all the tools and it is only a matter of applying himself and not getting fatheaded."[33] It was almost as if Schmidt inherited Allen's legacy. In that sense, it was Schmidt's good fortune that the Phillies acquired the enigmatic slugger when the young All-Star's career was at a critical juncture.

"Growing up," said Schmidt, "I admired Dick Allen. I pretended I was like him when I was up at bat playing Legion ball in Ohio. I was fortunate that we became good friends on the Phillies and that I learned a lot from him."[34] Allen would help Schmidt learn to cope with the press, the boo-birds, the fickleness of Philadelphia baseball itself. He was really the only person who could, having experienced it himself six years earlier.

"Schmidt had as much talent as anybody I've ever seen play the game," said Allen of his younger teammate. "Quick wrists. Strong. Perfect baseball body. But he was trying to hit every pitch out of the park, and when he didn't, he'd sulk about it. When I got to Philly in '75 he didn't seem to be playing the game. I talked to him about swinging down on the ball. The downswing is the ticket. Schmidt picked up on it pretty quick. The other thing about him was his attitude. He was moody and if he had a bad game, he'd take it home with him. I used to take him out after a game for a couple of beers and we'd talk about things, have a few laughs, put the ballyard behind us. I used to tell Schmitty to pretend he was back in the sandlots of Ohio where he grew up. Get out there and bang that ball like you did in high school. He began to get the message. He hit 38 homers in 1975 but struggled with his average. He still had some work to do."[35]

Like all prodigious power hitters, Schmidt continued to battle the strikeout. As much as he was revered for his ability to hit the home run, he struggled to become a better hitter. His statistics over the previous three years reflected the severity of the problem. In 1973, his rookie year, Schmidt hit 18 home runs, batted a career-low .196 and struck out 136 times in 367 plate appearances. The following year he led the league with 36 homers, improved his average by nearly 100 points, batting .282, but also continued to lead the league in strikeouts with 138. In 1975, Schmidt's home run production increased to 38, but his strikeout total jumped to 180, and his average dropped to .249.[36] The frustration began to mount, not only for Schmidt but for Ozark.

Near the end of the 1975 campaign, as the Phillies and Schmidt found themselves floundering in a two week slump, Ozark was asked about his struggling slugger. "He's not doing himself any good, he's not doing the club any good, and if he doesn't get going soon he's going to be out of a job," he replied in his characteristically unemotional manner. "He started off bad and instead of getting mad, gritting his teeth and working harder, he began fighting himself. And thinking. He's thinking all the time. Now he's so confused he doesn't know what to do. And to top it off, I think he's scared of the ball. In this business, if you're scared of the ball, you've had it. I'm really afraid for him. And the management here feels the same way."[37]

Ozark's frustration was understandable. He was the manager of an awesome team that featured both 1974 home run champions (Schmidt and Allen), two former Cy Young Award winners (Carlton and Lonborg), the best second base–shortstop combination in the game (Cash and Bowa), a top-notch bullpen led by newly acquired Tug McGraw, and a quality bench. Of the 24 major league teams, only Cincinnati and Oakland could match the Phillies in terms of all-around talent. Yet the Phils couldn't put it all together. With a week remaining in the season they were 6 and a half games behind the Pittsburgh Pirates in the National League East, heading for a second-place finish. Schmidt took the brunt of the criticism. Ozark dropped him from third to sixth in the batting order and began to question his intensity. The Philadelphia press chimed in, nicknaming him "Captain Cool." And the fans booed him mercilessly.[38] Through it all, the young third baseman kept his outward composure, though it was tearing him up inside.

"Our fans overreact both ways," he observed. "When you're in a slump, they're brutal, and when you're going good they make you come out of the dugout and tip your cap for every little thing. They're so passionate, it scares the hell out of me. You're trying your damnedest. You strike out and they boo you. I act like it doesn't bother me, like I don't hear anything. But the truth is I hear every word and it kills me."[39] If Schmidt was bothered by all the booing or those occasions when he failed to deliver in the clutch, why didn't he show it? Why didn't he get visibly angry, kick a water cooler, or pick a fight with an opposing player? When asked why he didn't show more emotion on the diamond, Schmidt simply replied, "What good would it do? The pitcher doesn't get me out. I get myself out. Nobody's got more natural talent than I do. One of these days, I'll put it all together for a whole season."[40] Unfortunately for the promising infielder, the immediate future would be more of the same rollercoaster of highs and lows.

Although the Phils' second-place finish in 1975 was a tremendous disappointment, there were some bright spots. Cash, Bowa, and Garry Maddox, the newly acquired center fielder from San Francisco, gave the Phils an excellent defense up the middle. Cash also contributed mightily to the offense, topping the National League in hits with 213, scoring 111 runs and batting .305.[41] In addition to Schmidt's 38 homers and 95 RBIs, Luzinski, who was rebounding from his injury of the previous season, contributed some formidable power with 34 homers and a league-leading 120 RBIs. McGraw went 9–16 with 14 saves out of the bullpen, establishing his role as closer. And journeyman outfielder Jay Johnstone found a home in Philadelphia's outfield as a platoon player with a reputation as a solid contact hitter.[42] What's more, the Phillies had a good mix of young ballplayers and seasoned veterans, all of whom were returning the following season.

Pitchers Tom Underwood and Larry Christenson were, at 22 years old, the youngest players on the team. Cash (28), Bowa (30), Luzinski (26), Schmidt (26), Maddox (26) and Boone (28) had not yet reached their prime. And Allen (35), Lonborg (33), Carlton (32) and McGraw (30) had had enough experience with winning to provide the kind of leadership necessary for a contender. The Phillies' exceptional combination of age, talent, speed, defense and power allowed them to dominate the National League in 1976, at least through the first half of the season.

The Phillies didn't seem to lose during the first four months of the 1976 campaign. At the All-Star break they held a commanding 10-game lead over the second-place Pirates. They had been playing .800 baseball since the beginning of June. Eleven of the Phils were hitting .300 or better. Carlton, who had been considered by many sportswriters as "washed up" after a 44–47 three-year slump, was 5–2, rejuvenated by the return of his close friend and personal catcher, Tim McCarver. Jim Lonborg, another former Cy Young Award winner who also suffered the same criticism, was 8–0 at mid-season and had pitched a near perfect game against the Dodgers. Together with Larry Christenson, Carlton and Lonborg combined to win 18 consecutive decisions. Not surprisingly, the Phils increased their lead to 15 and a half games by August 1st. Thomas Boswell of the *Washington Post*, one of the more astute baseball writers, stated that the Phils were "on the sort of natural, unrealistic high that blesses a team perhaps once every 20 years. They can beat you every way: power, hitting for average, speed, defense, and brains."[43]

Schmidt's bat was at the heart of the Phillies' success. His hot hitting began in a mid–April contest against the Cubs at Chicago's Wrigley Field. Schmidt had been struggling at the plate through the early spring. The harder he pressed, the less success he had. Ozark tried to break the slump by hitting the free-swinging Schmidt out of the lead-off spot, believing that the third baseman would be forced to take more pitches. It didn't work. To make matters worse, Rich Ashburn, a former Phillie great, broadcaster and writer for the *Philadelphia Bulletin*, was highly critical of the manager's strategy in his column. Ashburn, who had tired of Schmidt's lack of discipline at the plate, suggested that he be dropped to the sixth slot. "You can take pitches there

On April 18, 1976, Schmidt holds four big bats, representing the four home runs he had hit the previous afternoon at Chicago's Wrigley Field. Those four homers made him the first National League batter in 84 years to hit four straight home runs in a single game. Note the curly 1970s hairstyle, also called a "perm." *(Courtesy of UPI/Corbis-Bettmann.)*

just as easily," he reasoned. "And if Schmidt happens to drive the ball, at least he has the chance to knock in some runs."[44] Schmidt read the column on the flight to Chicago, and a shouting match erupted between the two men. As it turned out, the altercation did more to break Schmidt's slump than anything else.

Ozark took Ashburn's advice and dropped Schmidt to the sixth slot in the opening game against the Cubs. It was a beautiful but windy spring day— a hitter's day at Wrigley. Before the game, Allen pulled Schmidt aside and offered some helpful advice: "Mike, You've got to relax. You've got to have some fun. Remember when you were a kid and you'd skip supper to play ball? You were having fun. Hey, with all the talent you've got, baseball ought to be fun. Enjoy it. Be a kid again."[45] Schmidt took the words to heart. He also made some other changes. Instead of using his own bat, he borrowed veteran Tony Taylor's, which was an inch shorter and an ounce lighter than his own. Terry Harmon, a utility infielder and fellow Ohio University alum, loaned Schmidt his tattered blue T-shirt for good luck with the tip that "it's got a lot of hits stored up in it."[46]

Carlton started the game but was knocked out in the second inning. Seven more pitchers followed in a slugfest that saw the Phillies trail 12–1 at one point. Schmidt put on an impressive display of firepower. After a fourth-inning single, he homered in each of his next four at-bats. Two of his home runs, a two-run shot in the fifth and a solo homer in the seventh, came off Cub starter Rick Reuschel. His third home run came in the eighth inning, a three-run shot off right-handed reliever Mike Garman. With the game tied 16–16 in the tenth, Schmidt came to bat again and nailed a Paul Reuschel fastball into the left field bleachers for his fourth home run. He became the tenth player in major league history to collect four homers in a single game.[47]

The Phillies' 18–16 victory went to Tug McGraw who pitched the eighth inning and surrendered two runs in the ninth to send the game into extra innings. Afterward, the comic reliever boasted, "Schmitty never would have done it without me!"[48]

Any other player might have taken advantage of the opportunity to criticize the manager for dropping him in the batting order, but Schmidt respected Ozark's decision. After the game he admitted that his manager "has a job to do and he can put people wherever he wants to." "If he wants to hit me third, I'll bat third," he added. "If he wants me sixth, I'll hit sixth. And if he wants me to bat ninth, then I'll bat ninth."[49]

Schmidt, who was locked in an early season competition for home runs with Dave Kingman of the Mets, went on a tear after that game. While Kingman hit six round trippers in a five-game stretch that April, Schmidt blasted seven in a four-game period. But he continued to battle the strikeout, whiffing a total of 12 times during that same streak. That is why he accepted Ozark's decision to bat him sixth. He agreed with his manager that his 1975 total of 180 strikeouts was "ridiculous." "No one with good hand-eye coordination like mine should strike out that much," he added. "If I swing as hard as I can swing, there are 90 times out of 100 I won't even make contact. Maybe I have one chance in 100 to hit it out. So why do I do it? If I were my manager, I'd fine myself $100 every time I pop up and give myself $100 every time I hit a ground-ball base hit. I just have to find what it takes to make me do what I know I have to do."[50]

Schmidt, at 26, continued to be his strongest critic. He took tremendous pride in his performance, but he never seemed to be satisfied with it. That kind of perseverance and his constant self-evaluation and dissatisfaction with himself and his abilities are the qualities that made him a great player. While Ozark and others in the front office were critical of Schmidt for being too cerebral, he wouldn't have had the success he enjoyed without being a perfectionist. What he needed to do to realize his full potential was to find the balance between the mental aspects of the game and his natural physical abilities, something that was easy to understand, but difficult to do. Schmidt realized the need for that balance in his approach to hitting: "I don't like to give pitchers much credit. I figure that 99 percent of the times I fail it's because of lousy hitting, not good pitching. I know that I shouldn't take a long stride and a big swing. I know I should just try to meet the ball. I know I hit most of my home runs last year with two strikes in the count, when I was protecting the plate because I was scared of striking out again. But knowing this doesn't always help. Sometimes when a pitcher lets the ball go, your mind goes blank. You just see the ball and you react the way you've trained yourself. The adrenaline starts flowing and you try to hit the ball a country mile to left field. It's really stupid, but that's the way it is. The truth is that pitchers aren't afraid of me. I'm a dangerous hitter, but I'm not a good hitter. I want to get to the level where I intimidate the pitcher, make him squeeze the ball when he sees me standing up there. I make a lot of money because I hit home runs. But deep down, I want to bat .340 some year."[51]

Schmidt and the Phils were coasting along through the 1976 season until September. Then they went into a three-week tailspin. They lost ten of their last 11 games while the second-place Pirates won 12 of their last 13. Their lead had dwindled to just three games by late September.[52] "It was a nightmare," said Schmidt. "The hate mail, the letters saying we were choking, the abuse. I'd be out there trying to catch a tough grounder, thinking that what I did would decide whether we'd be two and a half in front the next day or four and a half. Blow this one, I'd think, and I'll need cops to guard my house."[53] Finally, on September 26th, in the first game of a double header against Montreal, Jim Lonborg pitched the Phillies past the Expos for a 4–1 victory to clinch the division.[54] It was the first time the Phils would go to postseason play in 26 years.

The Phillies faced Cincinnati's Big Red Machine in the National League playoffs. The Reds had an intimidating lineup with Pete Rose, Joe Morgan, Johnny Bench, George Foster, and Tony Pérez. They also had experience in postseason play, having won the World Series in 1975 and making regular appearances in the playoffs earlier in the decade. But the Phillies, who had won eight of the twelve regular season contests against the Reds, had the kind of team that could dominate a short, three-game series. They had stronger pitching with a rotation that included Carlton (20–7, 195 Ks, 3.13 ERA), Lonborg (18–10, 118 Ks, 3.08 ERA), Christenson (13–8, 54 Ks, 3.67 ERA) and Underwood (10–5, 94 Ks, 3.52 ERA). They also had comparable power in Schmidt (.262 avg., 38 HR, 107 RBIs), Luzinski (.304 avg., 21 HR, 95 RBIs), Allen (.268 avg., 15 HR, 49 RBIs) and Maddox (.330 avg., 6 HR, 68 RBIs).[55] But the Reds' depth and postseason experience proved to be too much for the Phils, who lost the playoffs in three straight games. Carlton was knocked out in the eighth inning of the opener at Veterans Stadium, which the Phillies dropped 6–3. In Game Two, Lonborg held the Reds hitless through the first five innings, but Cincinnati launched a 4-run attack in the sixth, sending him to the showers with a 6–2 loss. The series moved to Riverfront Stadium for Game Three. Jim Kaat started for the Phillies and was spotted a one-run lead in the fourth on doubles by Luzinski and Schmidt. The Phils increased their lead by two runs in the seventh on a walk and doubles by Schmidt and Maddox. Kaat was relieved by Ron Reed in the seventh, who surrendered four Cincinnati runs. The Phils came back in the eighth scoring another three runs and giving Reed a 6–4 lead going into the ninth. Unfortunately, the Phils would lose the game 7–6—and the pennant—on home runs by Johnny Bench and George Foster.[56]

Despite the Phillies' success on the playing field, there were signs of racial turmoil in the clubhouse. Once again, the controversy seemed to center on Dick Allen. Bowa constantly criticized the first baseman's inability to dig balls out of the dirt, something Allen's predecessor, Willie Montañez, could do with great skill. Allen confronted the antagonistic shortstop, telling him to make more accurate throws. At the same time, Allen, by early August, had begun to question the equity of Ozark's platoon system in the outfield. He believed that the black players Ollie Brown and Bobby Tolan were not "getting the shot they deserved" and that the Phillies were "working a quota system."[57]

Matters became worse as the Phillies' losing streak mounted in September. It appeared as if there were two teams—one white, the other black. Just before the Phillies clinched their division, management announced that they had to cut the postseason squad to 25 players and that veteran Tony Taylor would probably not be eligible for the playoffs. Taylor, a scrappy Cuban-born infielder and a fan favorite, had played with the Phillies for 15 seasons and had never made it to the playoffs. Allen was furious. He was a close friend of Taylor's, having known him since the mid–1960s when they came up together in the Phillies organization. "To my way of thinking, nothing could be more unfair than for the Phillies to take Tony Taylor's uniform," he fumed. "He played 19 seasons in the big leagues, but never in a World Series. He was a model player in the Phillies organization, mostly through the club's worst times. He was the one guy that would walk to the box seats and sign autographs before every game. He was the one guy who would volunteer to do a post-game interview when the rest of us were turning our backs on the press. In all his years, he never complained. Tony Taylor was Philadelphia Phillies baseball."[58]

Allen took the snub personally, and he gave the Phillies an ultimatum: unless Taylor was made eligible, Allen would refuse to play in the postseason. "With God as my witness," he told the front office, "if you take Tony Taylor's uniform off his back, you'll have to take mine too."[59] It was no idle threat. Allen desperately wanted a World Series ring, but it wasn't going to be on a racially divided team. The Phillies eventually agreed to keep Taylor in uniform for the playoffs, but placed him on the roster as a coach.

After the Phils clinched their division in Montreal, Schmidt, Allen, Cash and Maddox gathered in an equipment room near the visitors' locker room while the rest of the team celebrated. Allen offered a prayer of thanks that the four players had shared the season together and then they joined their team-mates' celebration. Some of the other players noticed their absence and complained about their "attitude."[60] Afterwards, the Phillies headed to St. Louis for their final regular-season series, and Allen returned to Philadelphia. He was mired in a slump and Ozark agreed to let him have the time off. When the press reported these events, they were less than complimentary to Allen. "To them, it was the re-emergence of 'Richie' Allen," said the Phils' first base-man. "I began to get booed, and the threats started coming to me in the mail. It was the 1960s all over again."[61]

Not surprisingly, Allen was released by the Phillies shortly after the playoffs. Dave Cash, who asked for and failed to receive a long-term con-tract, became a free agent and was eventually signed by the Montreal Expos.

While there were those who interpreted Schmidt's friendship with Allen and Cash, as well as the perm hair style he wore during the mid–1970s, as a rejection of the organization's poor treatment of its black players, Schmidt denies that he was making any political statement. "Sure, I may have confided in Dave Cash and Dick Allen," he admitted, looking back on the early part of his career. "I respected their playing abilities, just as I did those of my other teammates. But that doesn't mean I was making a statement about race rela-tions on the Phillies. Sure, I heard Dick talk about his experience in the minor leagues and having to stay in a separate hotel. Like anybody else—white or black—I felt badly for him that he had to deal with that kind of discrimina-tion. But I never donned a curled hair style—or what some called a 'red Afro'—to show my sympathy for the blacks on the team. In fact, many white players wore that kind of hair style in the 1970s. Bud Harrelson of the Mets was the first to try it out and I was the second. It was a practical thing to do. You didn't need to blow dry your hair after a shower! It had nothing to do with the black athletes on the team."[62]

Ultimately, the color of a player's skin didn't matter to Schmidt. What mattered to him was the way he played the game and how he treated his team-mates. Whether consciously or not, Schmidt made an earnest effort to tran-scend racial differences, judging a man by his character rather than his skin color. He treated his teammates as human beings, first and foremost, just as he wanted to be treated himself. Trusting of others, sometimes to a fault, Schmidt possessed a refreshing innocence when it came to race relations. It was difficult for him to understand why the sportswriters made such an issue of it. "The baseball writers used to claim that Dick would divide the club-house along racial lines," said Schmidt near the end of his career in 1988. "That was a lie. You walk into any major league clubhouse today and you'll see the white guys at one end listening to their music and the black players listening to theirs. It was that way in Dick Allen's era, and it's that way today. In all my years, I've never seen it different. The truth is that Dick never divided any clubhouse. He just got guys thinking."[63]

Although he was one of the most controversial players in Phillies history, Dick Allen left an important legacy. He forced Philadelphia baseball and its fans to come to terms with the racism that existed in the city during the 1960s and 1970s. He may not have done it with much self-discipline or tact, but he did pave the way for mutual respect between the city's black athletes and the white-run sports franchises for which they played.

Chapter Three

From Home Runs
to Humility

By the age of 27, Mike Schmidt appeared to have it all. In March of 1977 he signed a rare six-year contract worth more than three million dollars, making him the highest-salaried player in the history of major league baseball. Having captured his third straight National League home run title and a second All-Star appearance, people began comparing him to Brooks Robinson.[1] He had a beautiful wife and a lovely home in Berlin, New Jersey.[2] For all his good fortune, though, Schmidt did not have peace of mind. He felt guilty for his affluence and professional success, struggling with the reasons for his good fortune.[3] Hoping to find some answers, Schmidt began attending Bible study classes that winter. It would be the beginning of a spiritual journey. The next two seasons would be a time of trial for him—a trial in which he would forge a strong spiritual faith and gain a better perspective of what was truly meaningful in his life.

Schmidt and the Phillies got off to a slow start in 1977, falling behind the division-leading Chicago Cubs, who dominated the early going. By late April, he was hitting an anemic .182 and three of his nine hits were home runs. Once again, Ozark grew tired of all the strikeouts. In one particularly dismal performance against the Pittsburgh Pirates, Schmidt whiffed in three straight plate appearances. There would be no fourth at-bat. Ozark lifted his young third baseman in the seventh inning for pinch hitter Jay Johnstone. "He was struggling and I thought I would put a better hitter up there with two men on in the eighth," Ozark said, explaining the move. "Jay Johnstone gave me a lot of clutch hits in the past as a pinch hitter."

When asked what the move would do to Schmidt's confidence, Ozark replied, "It might ease things for him. He might come back tomorrow with a different attitude. This could make him a bigger man than he is."[4] Once again, Ozark was delivering his point through the press. It wasn't a good strategy if he wanted to win over the allegiance of Schmidt, who was very sensitive about his poor showing and tended to place even more pressure on himself than his manager. In fact, Ozark was trying too hard in his awkward attempt to motivate Schmidt. Clearly Ozark recognized his slugger's tremendous potential. Perhaps he even deluded himself into believing that he could establish a place for himself in baseball history by cultivating that potential. But it didn't work. If anything, Schmidt had grown accustomed to his manager's criticism. "Hey, we've only played 13 games," he said to the press, being as diplomatic as possible. "I haven't batted 50 times yet. Besides, my teammates have confidence in me. I know that much. They've seen me strike out three times in a row and then hit a home run. That could have happened tonight, if I had that fourth at-bat. But I can't second-guess the manager. Maybe if I was in his position, I would have done the same thing."[5]

By mid–June the Phillies had rediscovered their winning ways and Schmidt, his home run stroke. The team climbed into second place with a 4–2 victory over the Atlanta Braves at Veterans Stadium. The fans had become less hostile in recent weeks, giving Schmidt a reprieve from all the booing he had endured earlier in the season. In fact, during a Father's Day game, a top-heavy exotic dancer by the name of Morganna Roberts bounced out of the third-base field boxes before the start of the second inning, wrapped her arms around the surprised third baseman's neck, and planted a kiss on his lips. Schmidt was speechless, being taken completely by surprise. But after the game he admitted that the fans could "boo all they want if they keep sending them out like that!"[6]

Although he had broken out of his slump, Schmidt wasn't satisfied with his performance. He wanted to become a *complete* player, more than a power hitter who put up big numbers. He wanted to prove that he could get on base and manufacture runs—and he did. Schmidt improved his ability to take pitches, working 108 bases on balls in 1974 to 112 in 1976. He also worked to become a threat on the base paths, swiping 23 in 1974, 29 in 1975, and 14 in 1976. While he admitted that he had made a name for himself as a home run hitter, the young third baseman realized that there were times he could "make a bigger contribution with a great defensive play or by stealing a base."[7] He began to realize those ambitions in 1977, until a brawl with Pirates pitcher Bruce Kison derailed his season.

Kison was notorious for hitting batters. In a July 29 game against the Phils, he nailed Schmidt in the ribs with a 2–0 fastball. Schmidt would usually shrug it off and take first base, as he did after getting hit twice in a recent series against the Mets. This time his patience was tested.

"Never come near me again or I'm coming—," he began to warn the skinny right-hander. But before he could complete the sentence, Kison interrupted: "What about now, big boy?"[8]

Schmidt charged the mound, and a bench-clearing brawl erupted. When the dust cleared, he had fractured the ring finger of his right hand, forcing him to miss the next three games. "It was a silly thing to do," Schmidt admitted afterward, "but there comes a time when you have to assert yourself. It gets to be a question of manhood. The fans must have been wondering how much I was going to take, and I'm sure my own teammates were wondering."[9] While Schmidt earned the respect of Kison, who saluted the Phillies' third baseman for "following up on his talk," the injury plagued Schmidt for the rest of the season, possibly costing him a fourth straight home run crown.[10] He also continued to struggle with the spiritual meaning in his life and took refuge in the Phillies' Sunday Baseball Chapel.

Baseball Chapel, a nondenominational Christian organization that arranges pregame Sunday services for both home and away teams in clubhouses across the nation, was founded in 1973 by Watson Spoelstra, a former alcoholic and baseball writer. Services were nondenominational and began and ended with a prayer. Speakers were enlisted from a church or parachurch organization such as Fellowship of Christian Athletes or the Moody Bible Institute. Each speaker was allotted 20 minutes and often addressed personal conversion experiences or brief explanations of scriptural passages. Most often a very simple theology was propounded, consisting of four tenets: (1) Jesus is the Son of God; (2) God and man are separated by sin; (3) Jesus is the intermediary; and (4) salvation is a matter of choice.[11]

Baseball Chapel was initially established to address the practical dilemma of how to provide ballplayers with the opportunity for religious fellowship on Sunday with the game's hectic schedule. Since Sunday games began at 1:00 P.M., most players arrived at the park by 10:00 A.M. to dress, stretch and take infield and batting practice. That left little time for church attendance. In 1973, only seven teams held a regular chapel service, but four years later Baseball Chapel had programs on all 26 major league teams, drawing more than 10,000 players, coaches, and clubhouse personnel. Not only was the organization scheduling Sunday services, but was also arranging Bible study groups. By the close of the 1980s, Baseball Chapel had expanded its program to more than 100 minor league clubs and had established itself as the major vehicle of the evangelical movement in professional baseball.[12] The dramatic growth of Baseball Chapel can be attributed to the increasing pressures of a changing sport and the players' need to find more stability in their lives.

Free agency introduced a narcissistic era in which many players defined themselves by how much they made rather than how they performed on the field. They challenged the authority of the manager, who earned only a fraction of their salary. Those players with incentive clauses were not shy about demanding more playing time so they could secure the bonus that came with so many more at-bats or innings pitched. Owners were also less willing to part with a highly paid player just because he bad-mouthed the manager or abused alcohol or drugs.

Just as the quest for money and power intensified, so did the players' pursuit of a fast-paced lifestyle. It was "macho," for example, to be sexually active. While there was nothing new about promiscuity in the major leagues, it became so prevalent during the 1970s that many wives resigned themselves to it or tried to block it out. During the season, players are on the road for two, sometimes three weeks at a time. Constantly pursued by fawning women, lonely for female companionship, players find the temptation for infidelity is great.[13]

Under such constant temptation and great stress to perform, many players began turning to Christianity in the 1970s. Some realized that they had achieved at an early age everything a young man could desire—money, fame, women—and yet there was still a sense of emptiness, or perhaps they saw faith as a solution to dealing with their fame and the extraordinary highs and lows of a very public occupation. The feeling of being unfulfilled led them to ask of born-again teammates: "How can I balance faith, family, and career?" "How can I not only survive in an intensely competitive career, but also prosper?" "How can I give back to the community?" Gradually these players overcame their doubts and, perhaps in a quiet moment, knelt and asked Christ to enter their lives. These ballplayers, now known as born-again Christians, accepted the full authority of the Bible and made a spiritual commitment to Jesus Christ, including the responsibility to witness their Christian faith to others.

Other players dedicated themselves to Christianity because of a severe crisis in their lives such as a serious drug or alcohol addiction, or a divorce. Still others took a more natural path to conversion. Those, for example, who had been raised in a strongly religious environment discovered both a natural attraction to the fellowship provided by born-again teammates and a meaningful way of dealing with adversity in their career. There were even those athletes who simply followed the crowd, not really committing themselves to faith but attending Baseball Chapel in the hope that it would give them better luck.[14]

For many Christian athletes, however, Baseball Chapel provided a regular fellowship that not only validated their faith, but gave them the strength to live by it. The influence of Christianity on a given team, however, depended largely on the number of born-again Christians in the clubhouse. The Phillies were among those teams on which Baseball Chapel exercised a great influence in the 1970s. Of the 25 players on the roster, 15 to 20 attended the weekly chapel service or took part in Bible study and fellowship.[15]

Encouraged by Bob Boone, who organized the services for the team, Schmidt began attending Baseball Chapel. "One Sunday I was coaxed into going to the chapel service," recalled Schmidt. "You have to remember that this was at a time when Baseball Chapel was considered taboo by many players. But the idea that a spiritual entity could take the pressure off of my life—that

God actually wanted to take the pressure off of my life—was extremely appealing to me. So my original desire for a spiritual relationship with the Lord was more selfish than anything else. I looked at it as an opportunity to take all the pressures out of my life and put them on the shoulders of Jesus Christ, allowing the outcome to be what He wanted it to be. That included everything, ranging from a dilemma in my personal life to going to bat with the bases loaded in the bottom of the ninth. After attending Baseball Chapel on that first occasion, I found myself reading scripture more and more and reflecting on my faith. It was the beginning of my spiritual journey."[16]

Initially, Schmidt relied on Baseball Chapel to give him the emotional strength to cope with a batting slump or the criticism of the fans. He also found fellowship with other Christian athletes on the team, including Boone, Jim Kaat and Garry Maddox.

Boone had been a close friend of Schmidt's since their days together in the Phillies' farm system. He was also developing an impressive career with the Phillies and, as a catcher, was by necessity a team leader. Kaat, a 39-year-old veteran who began his major league career in 1960 with the Washington Senators, arrived in Philadelphia in 1976. He was a solid relief pitcher and spot starter who was on his way to an 8–5 record that season. Kaat credited his longevity and his success in the big leagues to his faith. He was one of the more active Christians in baseball during the 1970s.[17] Maddox had been with the Phillies since 1975, earning a reputation as the finest defensive center fielder in the game. Known around the National League as the "Secretary of Defense," Maddox, like Schmidt, had a reserved disposition, was always working to improve his performance, and was never satisfied with his game. A deeply religious man who relaxed before games by reading the Bible, Maddox converted to Christianity as the result of his experience as a soldier in Vietnam.[18] He and Schmidt became the closest of friends, traveling together to the ballpark each day, studying scripture, and spending their free time with each other.[19] Boone, Kaat and Maddox were admired by their teammates not only for their talent, but for their quiet honesty and humility.

Throughout his trying season, Schmidt had several "rap sessions about religion" with his Christian teammates. They spoke with him about how accepting Christ into their lives helped them with the constant pressures and materialism of major league baseball. Schmidt considered the three players the "best examples of Christian athletes in the game" and trusted them completely with his own spiritual dilemma. Over the course of the next two seasons, Boone, Kaat and Maddox would help Schmidt understand that being a Christian "doesn't guarantee clear sailing all the time." They reminded him that he had "put the worship of God above 'success.'" Of greater importance was "having a personal relationship with Christ." If the talented third baseman truly believed that "Jesus Christ was living inside of him" and that he was "doing everything for Him and through Him, then the burden of life in general [would] be lifted" from his shoulders.[20] Their fellowship seemed to help Schmidt as he continued to face adversity in his career.

On August 5, the Phillies battled their way into first place in the National League East by a half game with a victory against the Los Angeles Dodgers. During the next two weeks they went on a 13-game tear, sweeping the Dodgers at Veterans Stadium, winning three more against the Expos at home and then traveling to Chicago where they won another four-game series. By the end of August, the Phillies had posted a 22–7 record for the month. They clinched the division on September 27 when Larry Christenson won his eighteenth in Chicago, 15–9.[21]

To be sure, the 1977 Phillies were one of the finest teams in the history of the franchise. They featured the National League's most potent one-two punch in Schmidt (.274 avg., 38 HR, 101 RBI) and Luzinski (.309 avg., 39 HR, 130 RBI). Free-agent Richie Hebner was signed to fill Allen's position at first base, and Ted Sizemore was acquired from the Dodgers to replace Cash at second. Along with Bowa, Johnstone and Boone, the two new infielders hit in the .280s, adding to the Phillies' deadly offense. Bake McBride, who was acquired from the St. Louis Cardinals in June, ignited the attack out of the lead-off slot, batting .339. As a team, the Phils led the National League with a .279 average and 847 runs. Their 186 homers set a new all-time mark in franchise history.[22] And the pitching was as formidable as the offense. Steve Carlton captured his second Cy Young, going 23–10 with 198 strikeouts and a 2.64 ERA. Christenson, posting a 19–6 record, enjoyed the finest season of his career. Lonborg contributed 11 wins, and Lerch another 10. And, with McGraw, Gene Garber, Ron Reed and Warren Brusstar, the bullpen was just as strong as the starting rotation.[23] But they just didn't have the postseason experience to clinch a pennant.

The Phils faced the Dodgers in the playoffs. Although the series opened in Los Angeles, many believed that if the Phillies could earn a split there they would be a cinch to win the pennant, having posted a 60–21 regular season record at the Vet. Carlton pitched the opener and enjoyed a 5–1 lead going into the seventh before the Dodger bats erupted to tie the score. But Schmidt broke the deadlock in the ninth on a two-run single, and the Phillies managed to hang on for the 7–5 victory, their first postseason win in 27 years. The Dodgers evened the series the following day with a 7–1 victory.

Game Three was played at Philadelphia's Veterans Stadium and would go down in the annals of club history as an all-time heartbreaker. The Phillies had a 5–3 lead going into the ninth. In the top of the inning, Gene Garber retired the first two batters and then surrendered an infield hit to pinch hitter Vic Davalillo. Manny Mota, another pinch hitter, followed with a line drive into deep left field. Greg Luzinski got a glove on the ball, but couldn't hold onto it for the final out. When Luzinski threw to second base, the ball hit a seam in the Astroturf and bounced into foul territory. By the time first baseman

Richie Hebner retrieved it, Davalillo had scored and Mota had hustled to third. Now the Phils were clinging to a one-run lead.

Dodger second baseman Davey Lopes followed with a hard liner to third. The ball hit off Schmidt's left arm and deflected to an alert Larry Bowa, who threw to first in a last-ditch effort to get the final out. Lopes beat the throw and Mota scored on the play, tying the game at 5–5. An errant pick-off attempt by Garber and a single by Dodger shortstop Bill Russell scored Lopes, giving Los Angeles a 6–5 lead that they preserved in the bottom of the inning for the victory. The Dodgers won the next night, 4–1, to clinch the pennant. Schmidt had a disappointing series, having just one hit in 16 at-bats for an .063 average.[24]

Shortly after the season ended, Andre Thornton, who had been Schmidt's teammate in Reading in 1971, paid Schmidt a visit that would have a significant impact on the third baseman's faith. By 1977, Thornton was playing for the Cleveland Indians in the American League, so the two men did not have many opportunities to visit with each other during the season. One evening, the two players and their wives got together at Schmidt's home. "Gradually the conversation turned serious," recalled the Phillies' slugger. "Andy brought up some of the very things that had been on my mind, such as why we should have been singled out for baseball stardom, and what it all meant—the prestige, the money, the sports cars. It didn't surprise me that Andy, a very devout Christian, related everything to his faith in God."[25]

The Thorntons also spoke of how much their lives had been blessed with their two small children, Theresa and Andy Jr., and about their hopes and dreams for them. The Schmidts, moved by their guests' openness, shared their desire to have a child of their own. "We talk about having it all," admitted Mike, "but there's one thing Donna and I don't have, something we've been denied—a child."[26] Andy Thornton was so touched by the admission that he bowed his head and offered a simple but beautiful prayer, asking God to give the Schmidts patience, understanding, and a child of their own. Within the next week, the lives of both men would change, dramatically. Thornton lost his wife and daughter in a terrible automobile accident, but he managed to survive the heartbreak and actually become stronger in his faith. Soon after hearing of Thornton's tragedy and the grace with which he accepted it, Donna learned that she was pregnant—another blessing for Schmidt. Again, he began asking himself what he had done to deserve it.

"Andy's example led me to think deeply about the kind of faith he had," said Schmidt. "I remembered the glow I'd seen on his face after he had told me about committing his life to Christ. I also remembered thinking at the time that he'd gone off the deep end. Now he was dealing so gracefully with the tragedy of losing his wife and daughter. How could he do it, if not for his faith?"[27]

Donna noticed the beginnings of a transformation in her husband's attitude toward life. "I think Mike was a little big-headed in those first years of his success," she confessed. "Not that he would strut around, but he was a bit egotistical, which all pro athletes are to some degree. He still had to come to terms with himself." Part of the dilemma was coming to terms with his faith, realizing that only part of his life was baseball and that there were more meaningful responsibilities he had to himself and to others.

"I was a Christian when we were married," said Donna, "but Mike struggled with his faith. It took him some time to realize that he is no different than anyone else in this world. That there is a God and a Christ and that you're not living for yourself, but for Him."[28]

Later that winter, Schmidt, still struggling with the meaning of his life, contacted Dr. Wendell Kempton, president of the Association of Baptists for World Evangelism. Kempton had been a speaker at one of the Phillies' Sunday Baseball Chapels and the slugger had been impressed with the evangelist's honesty and dynamism. He began meeting with the Schmidts on a regular basis for Bible study. The sessions proved to be fruitful and on January 9, 1978, Schmidt dedicated his life to Christ. "I was alone in our bedroom and I came across a pamphlet called 'The Sinner's Prayer,'" he remembered. "I started to read it, then I began to say the words out loud, then, little by little, those words became my words. I acknowledged my flaws. I acknowledged my need of Jesus. I asked Him to come into my life and be my personal Saviour. It didn't come out of a tragedy. No fireworks went off. But I decided that I ought to turn over the reins of my life to Jesus after all He had given to me."[29]

In February, Schmidt left for the Phillies' spring training camp in Clearwater, Florida, a new man. He was convinced that 1978 would be a banner year for him. His optimism was reinforced by Ozark, who named him team captain that spring. Then, when the Phillies broke camp and headed North, Schmidt's fortunes began to change. He suffered a severe pull to a rib cage muscle during the first week of the regular season. The injury put him on the disabled list for three weeks. After he came off, he wasn't able to play without pain for another two weeks. By June, Schmidt was pressing, trying to make up for lost time. He was showered with boos on a regular basis and the more he pressed, the worse he seemed to perform. Despite all the negativism of the Phillies' fans, the third baseman never made excuses for his performance. He played through nagging injuries that season and never let up. He also tried to put the fans' criticism into a proper perspective. After one particularly frustrating series against the Mets in late August, he admitted that he "deserved to be booed." He even confessed that, "If I had a 'boo' sign in my back pocket, I would pull it out and join them!"[30] Although Schmidt had become diplomatic towards the boo-birds, it was more difficult for his wife. "It wasn't just the booing," she recalled; "it was the cruel things they'd say. Nor did they limit their criticism to Mike. I remember one occasion when I was pregnant for the first time, an emotionally trying time for any woman. I was at the ballpark and this fan kept saying how ugly I was. The tears welled up in my eyes. I stayed away from the park for a long time after that."[31]

The 1978 campaign was a trial for Schmidt. Because he accepted Christ into his life, he believed that personal and professional success was assured. He discovered, however, that there was much more to faith than the initial commitment. Bible study sessions with Kempton became more frequent. "What's this all about?" Schmidt demanded to know. "I become a Christian and this is what happens?" Kempton reminded him that faith is a journey, not a destination. That if he genuinely and willingly gave himself to God that He will always be there to support him, win or lose. "Mike, when you go to bat, tell the Lord outright that you're going to give Him one hundred percent," suggested the Baptist minister. "If you strikeout, you'll strike out doing your best. If you get a hit, that'll be doing your best too. Put the outcome in His hands."[32]

Kempton was emphasizing the importance of the "Try Ethic," a philosophy rooted in 1 Corinthians 9: 24–27 and adopted by Christian Athletes. Years later, Schmidt would explain it as "the idea of being a winner whether you win or lose as long as you give everything you have." Kempton's advice to place the outcome in Christ's hands allowed Schmidt to let go of the pressure he felt of having to control each at-bat or, in a larger sense, the outcome of the game itself. He gradually came to accept that he could only control certain things, like his "fear of failure, metabolism, and mindset by placing all the pressure on Jesus Christ." Other things, such as whether or not he got a hit, were beyond his control.[33]

At the same time, Schmidt was also discovering that the born-again movement had its detractors among the players and the media. It was not uncommon, for example, for teammates to charge that the commitment to Christ lessened the intensity a born-again carried onto the playing field with him, or to question whether he was trivializing religion by attributing his on-field performance to it, the assumption being that a born-again Christian asked God for victory. The media proved to be most skeptical of the evangelical movement, tending to cast Baseball Chapel as a misguided use of religion by a cadre of athletic groupies who call themselves "ministers." Team chaplains were portrayed as little more than good-luck charms who misused religion by worshipping sport and the players as much as Jesus. Their call for religion was superficial, critics claimed, because their real focus was on winning and had little to do with faith at all.[34] Schmidt would have to give serious consideration to whether he wanted to be associated with a movement that bred such hostile criticism. Would the spiritual peace of mind he sought be worth the price of further scrutiny by the fans and the media?

Schmidt was not able to regroup from the early season injury, and his statistics dropped significantly from previous years. He finished the 1978 campaign with a mediocre .251 average, 21 home runs, 78 RBIs and just 129 hits in 513 at-bats. He also struck out 103 times. Nevertheless, the Phillies' 90–72 record, though not as impressive as the previous season's, gave them a one and a half game lead over the second place Pirates and another playoff berth. Unfortunately, the team's postseason jinx continued as they dropped the playoffs, once again, to the Dodgers. With the exception of Game Three, in which Carlton breezed to a 9–4 victory, the Phils came up losers. The most heartbreaking contest came in the fourth and final game when the Phils lost on a Garry Maddox error in the 10th inning, 4–3. Again, Schmidt's performance was below par. He went 3 for 15 with two doubles, compiling a .200 average for the series.[35] The offseason would prove to be more fulfilling.

Shortly before Christmas, Donna gave birth to their first child, a daughter named Jessica Rae. Schmidt was awed by the experience. There he stood in the delivery room of the hospital in surgical garb, tears of joy welling up in his eyes, watching his wife give birth to their first child—a child he thought they might never be able to have. When the doctor placed the baby girl in Schmidt's arms, everything seemed to fall into place. All the booing, the strikeouts, the criticism of the press were inconsequential at that moment. Even his baseball successes—the home run titles, the All-Star appearances and the multimillion-dollar contract—paled in comparison to that moment. Because in that unforgettable moment, Mike Schmidt "knew for certain that life wasn't about money or status or cars, or even baseball stardom. It's about loving God, serving others; it's about families and husbands and wives loving and respecting one another; and it's about having kids to love and raise."[36] Although such a realization might seem instinctual to others, it is a very difficult one to grasp for a professional athlete who achieved so young the kind of stardom and fame that Schmidt had.

Perhaps Schmidt had simply begun to take his successes in life for granted. He often admitted that he had led a "charmed life." He was raised by a supportive, loving family who gave him all the advantages of a stable home life. With the exception of a dismal rookie season, his baseball career had been an uninterrupted string of successes. He enjoyed affluence that few players of his era would ever know. Predictably, he had been all-consumed with himself and his career.

"I had always been out for myself, for number one," admitted Schmidt. "I was willing to advance at the expense of others, do anything to get to the top, to the majors, to wealth. That was the kind of competitive attitude you had to have to be successful as a pro athlete. Ironically, it was that kind of selfishness—the idea that I could now go to home plate and succeed because I'm a Christian—that motivated my initial desire for a spiritual relationship with Jesus Christ. I was fortunate that my introduction to Christ wasn't the result of a serious problem with drugs, alcohol or illness. As I grew, as I read the Bible and met other Christians, and as I became less selfish, my faith in Christ became everything in my life. So I really have to give people like

Watson Spoelstra credit for creating Baseball Chapel, because it allowed me to accept Jesus Christ into my life and that, of course, has made a profound difference for me."[37]

For many professional athletes that "difference" is often characterized by an overwhelming sense of humility. Humility is, after all, the most difficult lesson to learn. Because the exceptionally talented athlete is pampered from an early age, his professional career is often marked by egocentricity. His ego drives him to pursue success for nothing more than its own sake, or possibly to discover just how good he really is. Often, the quest borders on extreme conceit or cockiness.

It would be easy to include Schmidt among the most exceptional—and most conceited—athletes. By the mid–1970s, the Philadelphia sportswriters had already dubbed him "Mr. Cool" because of the seemingly effortless way he played the hot corner and his extraordinary ability to control his temper on the playing field.[38] In Philadelphia, where fans expect their players to be rough-and-tumble, "cool" is not a complimentary term. Additionally, Schmidt's reserved but intimidating demeanor suggested to fans that he was at best "aloof," at worst, "cocky." Compared to such egotistical players as Willie Montañez of the Giants, Reggie Jackson of the Orioles and Gary Carter of the Expos, however, Schmidt was downright humble. He was quick to give credit to his teammates or to the opposition when he genuinely felt they deserved it. Nor did he boast about his achievements or flaunt them in front of others. If Schmidt exuded confidence on the playing field, then it was probably his attempt to compensate for the lack of confidence he had in his own ability to meet the demands of the Phillies' faithful.

Schmidt, then, was self-absorbed, not cocky. Meticulous to a fault, he went to extraordinary lengths to prepare himself mentally and physically to play the game. He trained year-round to stay in peak performance. He endlessly studied the opposing pitchers and their repertoire. On the road, he was known to take his bat back to the hotel room and practice his swing in front of the mirror, especially when mired in a slump. All of these measures reflected the tremendous pride he took in his performance. The catcalls, jeers, and boos from the stands only made him push harder. Ultimately, the pressure of it all led him to seek refuge in Baseball Chapel. There he found a deeper spiritual meaning through prayer, meditation, Bible study and worship by joining in fellowship with like-minded players.

Like all Christian athletes, Schmidt came to understand that accepting Christ into his life did not mean that he was infallible. While he would continue to make mistakes in his life, his spiritual commitment gave him the courage to admit those mistakes and to rectify them.[39] Thus, the trials he experienced on the playing field, his struggle with his faith and the birth of a beautiful, healthy daughter, enabled him to gain a better perspective on his life. These experiences gave him a powerful sense of selflessness essential for a genuine faith in God. That selflessness allowed him to realize his truly meaningful responsibilities as husband, father, and public role model.

With his newfound faith, Schmidt became more giving of himself to others. He became active in community service, his initial involvement coming through the Christian Children's Fund, which sponsors underprivileged children in third-world countries. Gradually, his concern for young people spread to a significant involvement with the United Way, for which he established a program that provided for corporate contributions based on the number of home runs he hit during several subsequent seasons. Later in his career, Schmidt helped other athletes organize similar programs in their own cities, accounting for one million dollars raised in Philadelphia alone and over two million dollars nationally. He raised funds for disadvantaged children in the Philadelphia area by serving on the board of directors of the Ronald McDonald House and the Philadelphia Child Guidance Clinic. Through the Mike Schmidt Foundation, he also established a scholarship program for students from Philadelphia's inner-city schools.[40]

Chapter Four

1980: A Career Year

Until 1980, the Philadelphia Phillies were the underachievers of major league baseball. Though they had tremendous potential with their mix of youth and seasoned veterans, though they had speed, power, depth and pitching, the Phils had no world championship to show for it. In three previous trips to the playoffs, the Phils had come up empty-handed. By now, the front office was growing just as impatient as the fans and the media. If the team could not deliver in the near future, chances were good that they would be dismantled, another one of the many missed opportunities in Phillies history.

Owens felt the pressure more than anyone else in the organization. As the Phillies' former farm director, he had signed and cultivated the nucleus of the club with such players as Schmidt, Bowa, Boone and Luzinski. As general manager, he had been responsible for engineering the trades that brought Garry Maddox and Bake McBride to Philadelphia.[1] In 1979 he would make two more transactions in the hope of capturing that elusive world championship. In February, he exchanged second baseman Ted Sizemore for the Cubs' Manny Trillo, another infielder who had originally signed with the Phillies in 1968.[2] But Owens' biggest catch came in March with the signing of free agent Pete Rose.

Rose and the Cincinnati Reds could not come to terms on a contract after the 1978 campaign, a season in which the 37-year-old third baseman hit safely in 44 straight games. The negative publicity over Rose's divorce from his first wife, Karolyn, was also a major factor in the Reds' decision to let their star player go.[3] Although several clubs entered the bidding war for Rose, Philadelphia held a special attraction for him. Rose considered Schmidt, the Phillies' marquee player, to be "the best in the game," one who was surrounded by some exceptional talent in Bowa, Luzinski and Carlton. He wanted to play for a winner, and he believed he could make the difference in the Phillies' quest for a world championship.

"I want to bring the world championship to a town that hasn't won it in half a century," said the former Red. "If I can get the Phillies to win the World

Series, I can do anything." Rose was only half joking. Just as important was his own desire to return to the Fall Classic, something he hadn't achieved since 1976, when the Reds won their last championship. "You have to lose a World Series before you realize how much you really wanted it," he confessed. "I keep telling the younger guys not to be satisfied with just being in the Series. I had to lose two in '70 and '72 before I found that out. Then we won two in '75 and '76 with Cincinnati." It wasn't that Rose didn't appreciate the personal successes—the batting titles, All-Star appearances, and hitting streaks— but that those things paled in comparison to winning the Series. "The statistics are just something that pile up over the years," he admitted. "You use those records as a way to motivate yourself day to day. But the only satisfaction that really stays with you is winning it all. After you've won the World Series, nothing else is enough. Frankly, it's all been disappointment since '76."[4] Because of the Phillies' potential to win a world championship and his personal interest in Schmidt's career, Rose rejected other, more lucrative offers to sign a four-year contract with the Phils worth $3.2 million.[5] For Phillies fans, the acquisition of Rose was almost too good to be true.

Pete Rose defined the game of baseball with his headfirst slides, blistering line drives, and a competitiveness that burned white-hot game after game for nearly two decades. His habit of running to first base on a walk earned him the nickname "Charlie Hustle," while his extraordinary hitting ability made for endless comparisons to Ty Cobb. Born and raised in Cincinnati, Rose cracked the Reds' starting lineup in 1963. Over the next twenty years, he proved that there was virtually nothing that he couldn't do well on a baseball diamond. He rarely made a mistake, whether he was playing second or third base or left or right field. He was the sparkplug of the heavy-hitting "Big Red Machine," leading them to pennants in 1970 and 1972 and to world championships in 1975 and 1976. In 1978 Rose enjoyed a 44-game hit streak, the last serious threat to Joe DiMaggio's 56-game record that clinched for the pure hitter a place in the game's history for him. Just as Schmidt would be named *The Sporting News'* "Player of the Decade for the 1980s," Rose had been the journal's choice for the 1970s.[6] Together with his cocky, almost combative disposition, Rose's exceptional talent made him easy to hate for Philadelphia fans. That is, until he became a Phillie. No wonder Mike Schmidt was able to refer to Rose as "the most likable arrogant person I've ever met."[7]

Growing up in Dayton, Ohio, Schmidt had been a Reds' fan, and Pete Rose had been his boyhood hero. Rose's uncle, Buddy Bloebaum, a scout for the Reds, was known to give Mike a few pointers on hitting during his high school days, emphasizing the mechanics that Rose had made popular as a switch-hitter.[8] Clearly Schmidt was ecstatic about the signing, though he downplayed it to the press. When asked if he thought Charlie Hustle's presence would inspire the underachieving Phils, Schmidt replied, "That's ridiculous and it isn't fair to Pete to expect that sort of thing. When a team doesn't live up to expectations, its natural to expect changes. This is simply one of those changes."[9] Perhaps he was trying to take the pressure off of Rose to make his boyhood idol feel more comfortable, but Schmidt welcomed another big name to share the limelight. In fact, one of the main reasons for signing Rose was to take some of the media pressure off the Phillies' third baseman.

While Rose certainly wasn't responsible for Schmidt's stellar play, he did guarantee the World Series credentials that set the third sacker on his way to Cooperstown. When Rose came to Philadelphia in 1979, Schmidt was a bona fide star, but one who had not yet reached the limits of his potential. Nor would his reserved personality and sensitive disposition allow him to enjoy the game. Rose took Schmidt to a higher level. He convinced him of his exceptional abilities, giving the young power hitter the confidence he needed to become the greatest third baseman ever to play the game. Rose's presence on the team and the press coverage he attracted took some of the attention and pressure off Schmidt, who became more relaxed and actually began to enjoy his successes. Rose had a special way of making the game fun for Schmidt. He nicknamed his younger teammate "Herbie Lee" after a boyhood friend. He boosted his spirits, getting him to laugh at himself on occasion, showing him that though Schmidt might be consumed by his love for baseball, he didn't have to take the game so seriously all the time.

"There's no doubt about it," admitted Schmidt, "Pete Rose had a tremendous influence on my career. He made a major difference for me and for the Phillies. You have to remember that from 1976 to 1978 our team captured the National League East title each season, but nothing seemed to go right for us in the playoffs. I'm not sure we knew how to win in that five-game, postseason series and it didn't matter if you won 100 games during the regular season—if you couldn't win in the playoffs, you were labeled a loser. The Phillies lived with that label until Pete Rose showed up. In 1980, Pete provided the kind of dynamic leadership that took the pressure off the other players. He was the finest team player I had ever seen. He always had something to say to pump you up, to play harder every game. At the same time, he was the kind of athlete who was boastful and could go out on the field and back it up. That allowed the rest of us to raise our level of play and, ultimately, go on to win the World Series."[10] But the world championship was still a year away.

The Phillies dropped to fourth place in 1979. Through the early part of the season, they looked unbeatable. On May 17 they won a 23–22 slugfest against the Cubs at Wrigley Field on a tenth inning homer by Schmidt. The victory gave the Phillies a 24–10 record and a four game lead in the division. Then their fortunes changed dramatically. They lost 16 of the next 21 games, falling to fifth place, seven and a half games out. Injuries had decimated the team. Trillo missed 46 games, having suffered a broken arm after being hit by a pitch. Luzinski missed 26 games with assorted leg problems. Boone was out

Pete Rose brought his headfirst slides, blistering line drives, and hard-nosed competitiveness to Philadelphia in 1979. The Phillies' only World Championship followed a year later. Schmidt credited the hustling first baseman with making a "major difference" for the Phillies and for his own career. (*Courtesy of Transcendental Graphics*.)

for 23 games, first with a broken finger and then an injured knee. Bowa missed 16 games with a thumb injury. In fact, Rose was the only regular who wasn't sidelined. By late August the Phillies had dropped below the .500 mark and were out of contention. On the last day of the month Danny Ozark was fired and replaced by farm director Dallas Green.[11]

A former major leaguer who pitched for the Phillies, Washington Senators, New York Mets and San Diego Padres, Green had worked his way up the ladder in the Phillies organization. After retiring in 1967, he managed two of the Phils' farm clubs, served as assistant director and, later, director of their minor league system. A self-confessed "screamer, yeller and cusser," Green was outspoken and harsh in his public criticism of the players. He conducted long workouts, stressed the fundamentals and had very little tolerance for what he perceived to be lackadaisical play.[12] Schmidt was diplomatic about the change: "I don't know if Dallas' screaming is all that significant. What is significant is that we're working harder and we're getting more accomplished. We'll execute better. We won't give as many games away. If he screams at me, more than likely, I'll deserve it. Besides, it doesn't hurt to get kicked in the rear end once in a while. It might just make me a better ball player!"[13]

Under Green, the Phillies completed the 1979 season by winning 19 of their last 30 games. Despite their fourth place finish, there were some bright spots. Rose was simply sensational. He played in all 163 games at first base (a brand new position for him), batted .331 (second best in the National League), collected over 200 hits for a record tenth time, stole a career high 20 bases and hit safely in 23 straight games. He also passed Honus Wagner as the National League's all-time singles hitter with 2,427.[14] Schmidt rebounded from a dismal 1978 season to set a club record with 45 home runs, which was good enough to finish second in the league in that category, while also collecting 114 RBIs. He also made an important change in his batting style that would eventually allow him to hit for average as well as power.

Although he had been a successful power hitter with his previous, slightly closed stance, Schmidt tended to pull the ball to left field. Throughout the season he experimented with different positions in the batter's box, finally settling on one patterned after two of the game's greatest hitters. "I wanted a stance that gave me a strike zone like Pete Rose's and that produced balls hit with power to all fields, much like the late Roberto Clemente," he admitted. "Clemente stood off the plate because he liked the ball out and away, on the outside corner. Having to force his upper body to go out after the ball was what felt right to him. The same is true for Rose, and I thought it would suit me best as a hitter too. So I backed up about eight inches off the plate and moved a bit deeper in the box. From that position, I could stride into the plate instead of striding toward the pitcher. That forced me to take my left shoulder into the ball, rather than to open up, allowing me to hit the ball more to center and to the right and left-center field gaps than down the left side."[15]

The adjustment enabled Schmidt to become more of a pure hitter, spraying the ball to all fields. At the same time he maintained his power, hitting home runs to right and center as well as to left field. By moving off the plate, he also became less vulnerable to the inside pitch, allowing him more decision-making time. It was the kind of change that would make a significant difference in his career, enabling him to stay at the top of his game while so many other sluggers tended to become one-dimensional hitters. In the future, Schmidt was able to have just as great an impact on the game by moving the runner, or by rapping a line-drive single, as he was by hitting the home run.

There is no coincidence that Schmidt made the adjustment in his hitting after Rose landed in Philadelphia. With the Phillies going nowhere in 1979 and Rose having removed some of the pressure on him, Schmidt felt more comfortable experimenting with his hitting style. At the same time, Rose encouraged him to think about the other facets of the game, not to limit his concern to his hitting. "Mike is human," said Rose during the 1979 season. "He slumps like anybody else. One time he was slumping pretty bad and I thought he was carrying that on to the field, not giving 100 percent at third base. I offered him a little advice: 'When you're not hitting, that's the time to work extra hard on fielding. You're doing nothing with the bat, but you can still contribute with the glove.'"[16]

Not surprisingly, during Pete Rose's five seasons in Philadelphia, Schmidt won the National League MVP Award two times (1980, 1981), the home run title three times (1980, 1981, 1983), the RBI crown twice (1980, 1981), the Gold Glove five times (1979–83), and was selected to the All-Star team all five seasons. "There are players who run faster, or hit for higher averages, or steal more bases," said Rose when asked to compare Schmidt to the other baseball superstars in 1980, "but he does everything. He's the best player in the game."[17] There was no denying that fact in 1980. It was not only *the* career year for Mike Schmidt, but the most memorable one in Phillies history.

The passage of time enhanced the glory of that season in Philadelphia. Most fans have forgotten that 1980 was not a "cake walk" for the Phillies. The team had to scratch and claw their way to the National League pennant almost from the start. No one expected the Phils to win their division. Even *Sports Illustrated* picked them to finish fourth.[18] Although Carpenter, Owens and Green believed that the team's poor showing of 1979 did not warrant a breakup, they did want to promote some of the top prospects in the organization. Those players included catcher Keith Moreland, infielder Luis Aguayo, outfielders Lonnie Smith and George Vukovich, and pitchers Dickie Noles and Scott Munninghoff. Additionally, Green, who had intended to return to the front office, decided to stay on as field manager that year, and Schmidt, who had been captain of the team since 1976, resigned the position, saying, "You've got Pete Rose, who exemplifies what a captain ought to be. Me, I'm a lot less outgoing."[19] Green accepted Schmidt's resignation, deciding not to fill the vacancy. "We don't have a captain because we don't need a captain," insisted the Phillies' outspoken manager. "What can a captain do besides take the lineup card to home plate? With my open door policy, I don't need a go-between. A player has every right to come in at any time and say, 'Skip, can I have a few minutes?' If you're gonna lay the authority figure on them or play God, you're gonna back some people off. I don't see the need for a captain on a veteran ballclub, other than Pete Rose, and Pete doesn't want the responsibility."[20]

A player strike canceled the final week of the spring exhibition season, possibly accounting for the Phils' poor start. April was horrendous. The pitching was mediocre at best, as Lerch, Ruthven and Christenson struggled to win a single decision. The hitting wasn't much better. Rose dropped below the .300 mark for the first time in years. Luzinski, Boone and Maddox were pressing to stay above .250. All things considered, the Phils were lucky to go 6–9 that month. But they seemed to turn the corner in May, posting a 17–9 record and taking a six-game win streak into June that put them in first place. But they ended up playing .500 ball for the rest of June and all of July, closing out that two-month period in third place, three games out.[21] Worse, a story in the *Trenton (N.J.) Times* on July 8 reported that Pennsylvania authorities wanted to question "at least eight members of the Phillies about allegedly acquiring amphetamine pills illegally from a Reading [Pa.] doctor." Schmidt was one of four players mentioned in the story, including Rose, Bowa and Luzinski.[22]

There was nothing new about drug abuse in baseball. It was a legacy of the excessive 1960s. By 1980, taking amphetamines to get "up" for games was a common practice. It helped to combat the fatigue of a grueling 163-game schedule in which players were constantly traveling from one city to another and, on many occasions, playing a day game less than twelve hours after the previous night's game had ended. Despite revelations that amphetamines were habit-forming and dangerous to the heart, many players defied the warnings and continued to abuse the drug as well as other painkillers and muscle relaxants.[23] Ken Moffett, director of the Players' Association, admitted that as many as 40 percent of major league players might be drug abusers. Over the next five years, the problem would reach serious proportions as revelations of drug abuse were made public among players in Kansas City, Los Angeles, San Diego and Pittsburgh.[24] But the allegations against the Phillies were largely unfounded.

After learning of the report, Ruly Carpenter immediately called a press conference and insisted that none of his players had "broken any laws" and that the allegations were "all speculative." Carpenter added that the Phillies had "continually cautioned their players against the use of drugs" and that the team's trainers did "not dispense drugs without a doctor's prescription." When Berks County district attorney George Yatron was questioned about the report, he admitted that an investigation had been underway for nearly a month prior to the newspaper story but that it "did not involve Schmidt or Bowa." He also mentioned that there was "no specific indication that any specific individual violated the law."[25] By mid–July most of the negative publicity had subsided, but the accused players were still bitter toward the media. Bowa refused to talk to the press at all. Schmidt found himself in a "limbo situation, trying to decide whether I owe anything to the media from now on after it has taken the liberty to tarnish my name."[26] On the field, the Phillies found themselves riding a roller coaster of wins and losses.

After being swept by Pittsburgh in an early August four-game series, Green locked the clubhouse doors and exploded at his team. They responded with a six-game win streak against Chicago and New York, cutting the first-place Expos' lead to just half a game.[27] Again they slumped. On September 1 after losing back-to-back games against the last-place San Diego Padres, it was Owens' turn to set the team straight. The Phillies general manager called a clubhouse meeting and laid down the law: "You guys played the first five months for yourselves. You've gone your own different ways. Your manager has been trying to get things across to you and now I'm telling you: 'Stop your Goddamned pouting!'"

Owens' patience had run out.

"I stuck my neck out after 1979 by refusing to break up this team," he bellowed. "I wanted to give you guys another chance! Now its my turn. The last month belongs to me and you had better deliver!"[28] The message was loud and clear—the Phillies had run out of "next years." There would be no future for the team if they didn't deliver a pennant.

The Phils won 19 of their last 25 games, as they exchanged first place with the Expos three times during that span. The contest that gave them the confidence to win in the postseason, however, came on September 29, the opener of a four-game series against the Chicago Cubs. In that game, the Phillies overcame a 5–3 deficit in the bottom of the fifteenth inning to win 6–5. "That was the first of many 'must-win' situations we faced," recalled Schmidt. "That was the first time we really felt like things had come together for us as a team." Having failed to deliver the winning run on two occasions in that game, Schmidt was especially grateful for the Phillies' new-found sense of teamwork. "In the past, it seemed that my teammates couldn't pick me up and the burden of failure would be even greater on me than anyone else in the same situation. But this time, Garry Maddox came off the bench to tie the game, and later, Manny Trillo won it. Those guys, picking me up the way they did made it possible for me to do some of the things I did against the Cubs later in the series, including two game-winning homers."[29] The Phils went on to sweep the series and headed to Montreal for a season-ending showdown with the Expos.

Montreal was an expansion club, coming into the National League in 1969. The organization had a short but hard-luck history. Until they finished second to Pittsburgh in the National League East in 1979, the Expos were largely a team of no-names. But now, under the leadership of a successful, experienced manager, Dick Williams, and such stars as Gary Carter, Steve Rogers and Andre Dawson, Montreal was a formidable competitor in the division. Of the 18 games the Phils and Expos played in 1980, Philadelphia won nine and Montreal nine. Ten of those contests were decided by one run. So the Phillies had their work cut out for them when they arrived at Jarry Park on October 3.

Dick Ruthven won the Friday night opener, 2–1, on Schmidt's forty-seventh homer of the season. Despite the flu, Schmidt was penciled into the lineup for the next day's game, which was delayed for over three hours by a steady rain. When the game finally began, it was a sloppy affair for the Phils, who committed five errors, four baserunning blunders, and hit into a center field-to-shortstop-to-third base-to-catcher double play. But the Phillies managed to survive their own foibles to win the game and clinch the division.

With the bases loaded and one out in the seventh inning, Greg Luzinski singled to center field, knocking in two runs for a 3–2 Philadelphia lead. On the hit, Montreal's center fielder Andre Dawson recovered the ball and caught Schmidt in a rundown between second and third. Shortstop Chris Speier tagged Schmidt for the second out and flipped the ball to third baseman Larry Parrish, who was covering second, to catch Luzinski. By the time the Bull was tagged out to end the inning, Montreal had recorded an 8–6–5–4–2 double play. The Expos took a 4–3 lead in the bottom of the inning, but Boone tied the game for the Phillies with a run-scoring single in the ninth. McGraw came in to pitch scoreless baseball, allowing only one base runner in his three innings of relief, setting up the climactic eleventh inning. Rose singled to lead off. McBride popped up. Schmidt, who had been battling the flu all game, came to the plate and hammered a 2–0 Stan Bahnsen fastball into the left field bleachers for a 6–4 Philadelphia lead, clinching the division and another shot at the pennant for the Phillies.[30]

Schmidt's home run, his forty-eighth of the season, set a new record for homers by a third baseman in a single season. It also capped a brilliant performance by the 31-year-old power hitter. In 1980, he captured his first MVP Award, leading the National League in home runs, RBIs (121), and slugging average (.624). His new batting style also allowed him to become a more complete hitter, as he raised his batting average to .286, the highest of his career to that date. But the Phillies' teamwork was also evident in the final statistics of other players.

The team's offense featured a number of consistent hitters, including McBride (.309), Trillo (.292) and rookie Lonnie Smith, who hit .339 and stole 33 bases in the 100 games he played that season. Although Rose dropped to .282, the lowest since his rookie year of 1963, he led the league with 42 doubles and played in all 162 games for the sixth time in his career. Luzinski

(19 HR) and Maddox (11 HR) added to Schmidt's firepower. Even the pitching, which had been so disappointing in the early going, was impressive during the final months of the season. Carlton's 24–9 record, 286 strikeouts and 2.34 ERA earned him a third Cy Young Award. McGraw was the National League's top reliever with 20 saves and a major reason for the Phillies' success down the stretch. After coming off of the disabled list on July 19, the comic reliever posted five wins and 13 saves, and his minuscule 0.52 ERA allowed the Phillies to win 12 of 16 one-run games in September. Two young rookie pitchers were also instrumental in the team's fortunes that season. Bob Walk won 11 games, and Marty Bystrom, called up on September 1, won all five of his decisions, surrendering just six runs in the 36 innings he worked that month.[31]

The Phillies' opponents in the playoffs were the Houston Astros, who clinched the Western division with a 7–1 victory over the Los Angeles Dodgers in an intradivisional elimination game. It would be the first appearance in postseason play in the franchise's 19-year history. Managed by Bill Virdon, who previously enjoyed success with the Pittsburgh Pirates and New York Yankees, the Astros featured such players as outfielders Jose Cruz (.302 avg., 11 HR, 91 RBI), César Cedeño (.309), and Terry Puhl (.282). First baseman Art Howe (.283) and veteran second baseman Joe Morgan (.243 avg., 11 HR, 49 RBI), who had come over from the Cincinnati Reds and was the only player who had any significant postseason experience, were also among the club's leading hitters. The Astros' pitching staff was even more formidable.

Joe Niekro (20–12, 3.55 ERA) was the ace of the staff. Nolan Ryan (11–10, 200 K, 3.35 ERA) was not yet a legend but was quickly becoming one of the most respected hurlers in the game. Ken Forsch (12–13, 3.20 ERA) and Vern Ruhle (12–4, 2.38 ERA) rounded out the starting rotation, while Joe Sambito was the stopper with 17 saves and a 2.20 ERA. Had J. R. Richard (10–4, 1.89 ERA) not suffered a near-fatal stroke in July, the Astros would have enjoyed even stronger pitching heading into the best-of-five-game series.[32] Still, the 1980 National League Championship Series proved to be the most eventful, if not most exciting, series since the divisional playoffs began in 1969.

The series opened in Philadelphia, where 65,277 fans packed Veterans Stadium to see Steve Carlton against the Astros' Ken Forsch. Carlton, who had not lost a game to the Astros in nearly two years, allowed only one run and two hits in the seven innings he pitched. But he did struggle with his control in the last few innings and was lifted for McGraw. Forsch held the Phils to four hits through five innings before Luzinski delivered the winning blow with a two-run homer in the sixth. Pinch hitter Greg Gross added an insurance run the following inning with an RBI single to left. McGraw silenced the Astros' bats for the remaining two innings for the 3–1 win. The victory was the Phillies' first in a postseason home game since Grover Cleveland Alexander defeated the Boston Red Sox in the first game of the 1915 World Series.[33]

Houston tied the series the following day when Nolan Ryan went to the mound. Ruthven, pitching for the Phils, surrendered only one run through six innings but became wild in the seventh, walking in another run before being relieved by McGraw in the eighth. Ryan surrendered two runs in the fourth, on doubles by Schmidt and Luzinski and a single by Maddox, and a third run in the seventh before being lifted. With the score tied at 2–2 and only one out, the Phillies loaded the bases. Sambito came in to strike out Bake McBride swinging. Then Virdon brought in right-hander Dave Smith to face Schmidt, who struck out looking to end the rally. The Phillies threatened again in the ninth. With one out, McBride, Schmidt and Smith loaded the bases on back-to-back singles. But Frank LaCorte came in to strike out Trillo and retire Maddox on a pop-up, sending the game into extra innings. Houston prevailed in the tenth when Jose Cruz singled in one run and pinch hitter Dave Bergman tripled in two more in a four-run outburst, giving the Astros a 7–4 victory.[34]

After a day off for travel, the series resumed at Houston's Astrodome on Friday, October 10. Larry Christenson faced knuckleballer Joe Niekro in a classic pitcher's duel. Christenson hurled three-hit shutout ball for six innings, while Niekro allowed six hits in ten innings of work. The Phillies were robbed of the winning run in the ninth. Maddox drew a two-out walk and stole second. Bowa was intentionally walked. Boone followed with a hard liner into the gap in left-center. But Jose Cruz, Houston's left fielder, sprinted to his left and speared the ball to end the inning. The Astros would not be denied. After working two scoreless innings in relief, McGraw was touched for the winning run in the eleventh when Joe Morgan tripled and Denny Walling sacrificed him in for the game's only run, a 1–0 Houston victory.[35]

Game Four proved to be the most controversial. Carlton went to the mound against Houston's Vern Ruhle. Lefty breezed through the first three innings, surrendering a run in the fourth and another in the fifth for a 2–0 Houston lead. The Phillies threatened in the fourth. With two men on and no outs, Maddox hit a soft comebacker to the mound. Ruhle fielded the ball and threw it to first baseman Art Howe. Then a 20-minute argument ensued. Home plate umpire Doug Harvey claimed that the Astros' pitcher had trapped the ball, but the first and third base umpires insisted that Ruhle caught the ball on the fly. Howe ran to second base to complete an apparent triple play. After Dallas Green protested the call, Harvey consulted with the rest of the umpiring crew and then with National League president Chub Feeney. When all was said and done, the umpires concluded that the Astros had turned only a double play, as time had been called when Howe attempted to make the third out. Following the ruling, both teams protested the game. Another controversy followed in the sixth inning. With a 2–0 lead and only one out, Houston loaded the bases. Astros catcher Luis Pujols flied to right. The runner at third, Woods, tagged and sprinted home. The Phillies' dugout erupted again, protesting that

Woods left too soon. On the appeal, umpire Bob Engel called Woods out. It was a critical ruling, giving the Phils the momentum they needed.

On the verge of another defeat, the Phillies rallied in the eighth inning. Pinch hitter Greg Gross led off with a single. Ruhle was lifted for Dave Smith, who promptly surrendered back-to-back base hits to Lonnie Smith, Rose and Schmidt, tying the game. Trillo sacrificed and Rose chugged home, crashing into Astro catcher Bruce Bochy. Bochy failed to handle the throw and Rose scored the go-ahead run. When asked after the game about the controversial play, Rose shrugged off any suggestion of foul play: "I was moving toward third and saw the coach wave me on. Bochy was concentrating on catching the ball. I was concentrating on scoring. That's the way the game is supposed to be played." "Besides," he added, "they made two bad relays there. The whole key was that the catcher didn't have the ball or he would have planted me."[36]

Houston tied the game in the home ninth, but the Phillies would not be denied. With one out in the tenth, Rose ignited the winning rally with a single to center field. Luzinski and Trillo followed with doubles, giving the Phils a 5–3 victory in one of the more controversial see-saw games of the series. At three hours and 55 minutes, Game Four was also the longest contest in playoff history to that date.[37]

Despite their come-from-behind victory, the Phillies were facing some tough odds going into Game Five since no National League team had ever won a fifth playoff game on the road. Additionally, the Phils were forced to start rookie Marty Bystrom against Houston's Nolan Ryan. The scoring started early. Houston took a 1-0 lead in the first on a single by Terry Puhl, who stole second and scored on Cruz's double. The Phillies took the lead in the second when Boone singled to center to score Trillo and Maddox. The Astros tied the game in the sixth on a two-base error by Luzinski and pulled ahead, 5–2, in the seventh on singles by Puhl and Walling and a bases-clearing triple by Howe. Once again, the Phillies had their backs to the wall but refused to die.

Bowa opened the eighth with a single to center. Boone followed with an infield hit. Then Gross laid down a perfect bunt to load the bases. After walking Rose to force in a run, Ryan was sent to the showers. Sambito came in to face pinch hitter Keith Moreland, whose bouncer to second scored another run. The Phillies had cut the Astros' lead to one run. With Schmidt coming to the plate, Astros manager Bill Virdon lifted Sambito and brought in Ken Forsch, who had had success against the Phillies' power-hitting third baseman earlier in the series. It was a key moment: Schmidt could make or break the Phillies in that single plate appearance. In a strange way, his career had come down to that moment. All the home run titles, the Gold Gloves, the All-Star appearances wouldn't mean a thing unless he could win a world championship. He was so close to that championship he could taste it. "All I had to do was hit a grounder to short and we would've won the game and the pennant," he said.

Instead, Schmidt struck out. "The good Lord proved something to me right there," he humbly admitted. "When I got back to the dugout, Del Unser hit a single up the middle, tying the game. I went 0-for-5 in that game. It's ironic that I had the year I had and now, when it means the most, I was completely humbled. My teammates did it all."[38] Trillo followed with a bases-clearing triple giving the Phillies a 7–5 lead. The Astros tied the game in the home eighth off Tug McGraw, but the Phillies would not be denied. They scored the run in the tenth when Unser doubled and Maddox followed with an RBI single to center, scoring his teammate with the winning run.

Dick Ruthven was called in to seal the victory. He retired pinch hitter Danny Heep on a pop-up to Bowa at short for the first out. Terry Puhl, who had already collected four hits, flied out to Maddox in center. Finally, Ruthven got Enos Cabell to lift a soft fly to center, and Maddox squeezed it for the final out, giving the Phillies their first pennant in 30 years.[39]

Although Manny Trillo, who batted .381 and starred defensively, was named the MVP of the National League Championship Series, the victory was truly a team effort. Phils owner Ruly Carpenter reinforced that fact during the clubhouse celebration that followed. "I'm tremendously pleased," he said in a characteristically understated manner. "What's especially nice is that I've never seen a series where so many people contributed to the victory. The fact that Garry Maddox got the game winner is the most satisfying of all because I know in the back of his mind and the fans' minds was the ball he dropped in the playoffs two years ago in Los Angeles."[40]

Schmidt agreed: "The playoffs showed we had become the kind of team that finds a way to win. Of course, we really had so much at stake in that series as well. After our previous playoff losses, we had to get over this hurdle and we did, overcoming everything from the umpiring to left-on-base records to win as a team. To be honest, I don't think we could have survived another playoff loss as a team. We were on the edge individually and as a team. The organization would have taken another direction had we lost. But we got over the hurdle. All the negatives of the years before were wiped out by winning the playoffs."[41]

The American League was represented in the World Series by the Kansas City Royals, a team whose postseason fortunes had paralleled the Phillies. Having suffered three playoff defeats in 1976, 1977, and 1978, the Royals finally won the American League flag in 1980 by sweeping the New York Yankees in three straight games. The Royals were loaded with talent. George Brett (.390 avg., 24 HR, 118 RBI) was the American League's best hitter. First baseman Willie Aikens (.278 avg., 20 HR, 98 RBI) also contributed some impressive firepower, while outfielder Willie Wilson (.326 avg., 3 HR, 49 RBI) and designated hitter Hal McRae (.297 avg., 14 HR, 83 RBI) were among the most consistent hitters in the league. Although second baseman Frank White and outfielder Amos Otis hit only .264 and .251 respectively during the regular season, their bats sparked the Royals to victory in the playoffs. White racked up a .545 average and three RBIs and Otis hit .333 and scored two critical runs. The pitching was every bit as impressive. Dennis Leonard (20–11, 155 K, 3.79 ERA) was the ace of the staff. Larry Gura contributed 18 wins, Paul Splitteroff 14 and Rich Gale another 13. Dan Quisenberry was the American League's top fireman with 33 saves and a 12–7 record as well as a 3.09 ERA.[42]

The Series opened on Tuesday night, October 14, in Philadelphia before a crowd of 65,791. Since the Phillies had depleted their pitching staff in the grind-it-out five-game series against Houston, Green was compelled to start his young rookie Bob Walk against the Royals' Dennis Leonard. The Royals pounded Walk early on a pair of two-run homers by Amos Otis in the second and Willie Aikens in the third. Just as they had done in the playoffs, the Phillies rallied in the bottom of the third. Bowa singled with one out, stole second base and scored on Boone's double to left field. Lonnie Smith followed with a single but was caught in a rundown as Boone scampered home with the second Philadelphia run. Rose was hit by a pitch. Schmidt walked. McBride then cleared the bases with a three-run homer over the right field wall, giving the Phils a 5–4 lead. The Phillies added runs in the fourth and seventh innings to give them a 7–4 advantage. It was barely enough. Willie Aikens hit another two-run homer in the eighth to cut the Philadelphia lead to one, but the Phils hung on for the 7–6 victory.[43]

Game Two was played the following evening and pitted Steve Carlton against Kansas City's Larry Gura. It was a scoreless pitcher's duel through the first four innings. Then, in the fifth, Keith Moreland ignited a two-run Phillies' rally with an infield base hit. Maddox followed with a double down the left field line. Trillo sacrificed Moreland home, and the second run scored on Bowa's base hit to left. Kansas City scored their first run in the sixth and took a 4–2 lead in the seventh but lost the game in the eighth when the Phillies blasted reliever Dan Quisenberry for four hits and four big runs to clinch the game. After Boone walked, pinch hitter Del Unser doubled home the Phils' third run of the game. McBride tied the score with a base hit to left field. Schmidt came to the plate next. He refused to fail in the clutch this time, jumping on Quisenberry's first offering for a double to right that put the Phillies ahead by a run. "I did not want to get behind him," he explained after the game. "Quisenberry is a one-pitch pitcher. He's got 33 saves and the best sinker in the American League. I guarantee you he's gonna throw me a good hard first pitch. That was what I was looking for and I got it."[44] Schmidt later scored on Moreland's single to center field for the 6–4 victory, and the Phillies went up by two games in the World Series.[45]

The Series moved to Kansas City for Game Three. George Brett, who was sidelined with a celebrated case of hemorrhoids in the previous game, returned to the Royals lineup, musing, "It's all behind me now!"[46] He went on to celebrate with a first-inning solo homer off Phillies starter Dick Ruthven.

The rest of the game was a see-saw battle in which the teams traded leads several times. Schmidt's solo homer in the fifth—his first homer ever in post-season play—was the silver lining in a game in which the Phils stranded 15 base runners and eventually lost 4–3. "The best thing is I only have to wait 10, 12 hours and then we play again," said Mike, bemoaning the loss. Not to detract from the Royals' hard-earned victory, he added: "I give them credit for coming back. That's why the Series is best four-out-of-seven, not two-out-of-three. There's enough time for the breaks to even out. Four-in-a-row hasn't been done in a long time. So we go out again tomorrow!"[47]

Larry Christenson started Game Four for the Phillies and never made it past the first inning, surrendering four runs and retiring only one batter. Dickie Noles, who relieved him, gave up a Willie Aikens' home run in the second before the Phillies put a stop to the Royals' scoring. But by that time it was too late. Kansas City went on to win the game 5–3 behind the brilliant pitching of Dennis Leonard and Dan Quisenberry.[48]

Manager Dallas Green selected 22-year-old rookie Marty Bystrom to pitch the fifth game of the World Series against 18-game winner Larry Gura. For three innings both hurlers held each other's teams in check. Then, the Phillies erupted for two runs in the fourth when Bake McBride's one-out bunt was misplayed by Aikens at first and Schmidt followed with his second home run of the Series. Kansas City finally scored in the fifth and added two more runs in the sixth to take a 3–2 lead that sent Bystrom to the showers. Quisenberry relieved Gura in the seventh, holding the Phils scoreless until the ninth. Schmidt led off that inning, ripping a bullet off of third baseman George Brett's glove. Brett's decision to cheat in a few steps because of Schmidt's bunt attempts in the first two games of the Series backfired. "I had no intention of bunting in that situation," said a surprised Schmidt after the game. "As a lead-off batter, I was just trying to drive the ball someplace. I did notice that Brett was playing me in, though. And maybe that helped me get on base. If he was playing me even with or just behind the bad, he might have had the time to make the play."[49] Schmidt scored when pinch hitter Del Unser doubled to right field. Moreland's sacrifice fly and Trillo's RBI single put the Phillies ahead 4–3. McGraw survived a shaky ninth in which he walked the bases loaded but still managed to seal the victory.[50]

On Tuesday night, October 21, the teams returned to Philadelphia for Game Six, which would prove to be the final game of the Series. Green called on his ace, Steve Carlton, while Royals manager Jim Frey chose Rich Gale. The Phillies began the scoring in the third inning. Boone led off with a walk. Lonnie Smith beat out a grounder and Pete Rose bunted to load the bases. Schmidt followed with a single to left field, driving in two runs. "I couldn't have gotten a bigger hit than that," he admitted years later. "I got the game-winning hit in the final game of the World Series. I was so excited that I even made a gesture—hoisting my fist into the air—when I reached first base.

Schmidt watches his two-run homer off Kansas City's Larry Gura leave Royals' Stadium in Game Five of the 1980 World Series. The Phillies went on to win, 4–3. (*Courtesy of Transcendental Graphics*.)

It was one of the few times that I found myself showing emotion on the field."[51]

The Phillies picked up two more runs by the sixth inning for a 4–0 lead. Kansas City managed to get a run back in the eighth off Tug McGraw, who came in to relieve Carlton. Ever the showman, McGraw provided ample drama in the ninth when, with a 4–1 lead, he loaded the bases with one out. Frank White then popped a foul down the first base side near the Phillies' dugout. Boone sprang out of his crouch, shed his mask and extended his arm to make the put-out. But the ball bounced out of his glove. Fortunately, Rose was there to grab the ball before it hit the ground. Now there were two outs.

Anticipating that the fans, who by this time had worked themselves into an uncontrollable frenzy, would launch a mad rush onto the field, the Phillies front office enlisted the aid of the city's police department. Mounted police and K-9 officers holding their German shepherds at bay formed a barrier along the first and third base lines to discourage any destructive behavior. With the crowd on its feet and cheering every pitch, McGraw struck out Willie Wilson to end the game.[52]

For a solitary moment, time seemed to stop. Amidst all the tears, laughter and sheer jubilation of the Philadelphia faithful was the realization that a miracle had happened—the Phillies had finally won their very first world championship. McGraw raised his arms toward the skies in victory and, turning to his right, looked to third base as Phillies converged on the mound from every conceivable direction. Just before the players could close ranks to embrace each other, Mike Schmidt, in a rare display of emotion, sprinted full speed to the mound and jumped atop the pile of his teammates. The monkey was off his back. Now he had it all. No one could ever take that world championship away from him.

Reflecting on the Phillies' world championship, Schmidt would later comment on the significance of that achievement in his own career: "Sometimes you'll hear one player saying about another, 'He's good, but he's never been on a winner.' You have to play to win. That's the one thing successful players share and that quality rubs off on the people around them—they reinforce each other. No matter how you perform individually, no matter how many home run titles you win, it means little if you're not part of a winning team. In Philadelphia and in my case individually, I didn't get that label until the 1980 World Series."[53]

Just as important was Schmidt's ability to deliver in the clutch. Prior to the 1980 postseason, he had been accused of failing to drive in runs when his team needed him most. But throughout the last month of the season, first in Montreal to clinch the playoff berth, and later in the Series, Mike delivered. "The last few weeks of the regular season as well as the World Series were special for me," he recalled years later, "because I put to rest any question about my ability to deliver when our team needed the big hit. 1980 was the year I was finally recognized as a clutch player."[54]

The following day more than one million Philadelphians turned out to cheer their Phillies as the team paraded down Broad Street to John F. Kennedy Stadium in South Philadelphia. There, 85,000 gathered to hear the players make speeches. "All through baseball history, Philadelphia has taken a back seat to New York City," said Tug McGraw, whipping the crowd into a wild frenzy. "Well, New York City can take this world championship and stick it!"[55]

Schmidt was predictably more humble. Moved by so many genuine expressions of kindness that afternoon, he took the microphone and thanked the fans for their support. "I never saw so many sincere faces in my life as I did in that parade today," he said, speaking from the heart. "Take this world championship and savor it. You all deserve it!"[56] Make-shift signs reading, "Mike Schmidt for President" could be seen dotting the parade route that day. All the criticism, the negative publicity seemed to pale in the wake of such a genuine outpouring of affection for the Phillies and their franchise player. Perhaps a love affair was beginning to blossom between Mike Schmidt and

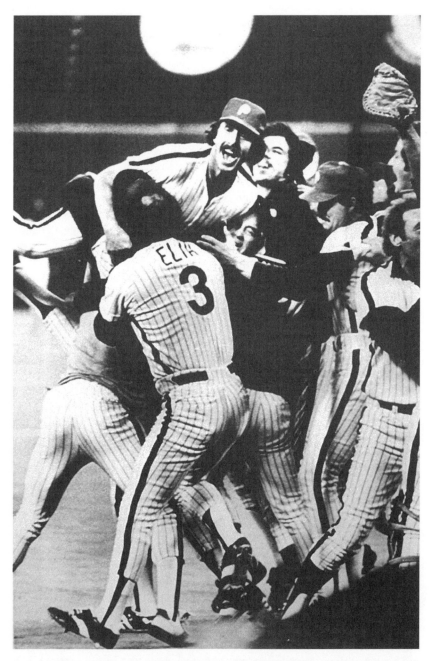

Mike Schmidt celebrates with teammates after the Phillies captured their very first world championship, October 21, 1980. He was later named the Series MVP for his .381 average, 2 HR and 7 RBI. (*Courtesy of Transcendental Graphics.*)

the baseball fans of the city. Or perhaps all the hard feelings were simply lost in the ecstasy and relief the fans had felt after being cheated out of "their due" for so many seasons.[57] For Schmidt, the world championship and the parade that followed had a deeply profound effect on his life.

"I had a great deal of fun playing in the World Series, because I let myself enjoy it," he admitted afterwards. "I let myself relax—I began to show more of the fun I have in a game, to have a smile on my face more often, to establish some rapport with the people in the stands."[58] He also spoke of his great admiration for his teammates: "The Phillies were such a good team in 1980 that when I or another player didn't come through, the guy that pinch-hit behind us did. Then, still alive in a game, we'd get a chance to redeem ourselves by getting the big hit in the next at-bat. We were playing to win and at the same time we reestablished the concept of a team. I was proud to be the goat of the playoffs because it gave some of my teammates a chance to be heroes. It's because I was part of something much bigger, part of a team, that this has been an unbelievable year in my life."[59]

After learning that he had been selected the MVP of the 1980 World Series, Schmidt downplayed his own contribution to the team and acknowledged Bowa's. "Larry Bowa had an outstanding World Series," he said of his teammate. "He could easily have been named the MVP. I guess they chose me because I had a little more notoriety during the regular season. Although I had 7 RBIs in the Series, Larry had two more hits than the eight I collected. He was also exceptional in the field. I'd have been just as happy if he had won the award."[60] In saluting Bowa, Schmidt had transcended the long-standing personal rivalry between the two players. It was a turning point in their relationship. Both men realized the significance of their contribution to the team and that the Phillies would not have won the Series that year had it not been for the two of them.

Later that year, Schmidt added another MVP to his trophy collection when the baseball writers made him their unanimous choice as the 1980 Most Valuable Player in the National League.[61] After learning of the decision, Schmidt first thanked "the good Lord" for his fortunes, then Pete Rose, and finally his grandmother Viola Schmidt. "Pete," he said, "instilled in me a new vitality for playing the game at this point in my career. Being 31 years old— which is a turning point for a lot of ballplayers—he gave me a great outlook on the game of baseball, a feeling of youth, and a feeling of wanting to have fun on the baseball field. Pete came along at a great time in my career and I'm thankful for that."[62] Finally, he thanked his grandmother who had died of cancer that September. She had been his biggest fan from the very start, playing baseball with him in the backyard when he was a very young child, altering his baseball uniform to his own liking when he was in high school, and sharing her love for Pete Rose and the Cincinnati Reds with him. Schmidt admitted that winning the MVP meant "a great deal to him" because he considered the award a tribute "to her interest and contribution to my baseball career." "I only hoped that she would hang on to see it happen," he added.[63]

At the same time, Mike seemed to come to terms with the meaning of baseball in his life. He began to see the game as a calling and his ability to play it a gift from God that would allow him to influence others—especially the young—in a constructive way. "I think the most rewarding thing for a person is to discover God's purpose for them and then to go ahead and act on that purpose to the very best of their abilities," he said when asked about his success that year. "To come to know what the Lord's purpose is for your life and then do it well, to give it all you have, is rewarding. Baseball is what God gave me—it's my purpose in life. Through that purpose, I have a chance to influence a lot of young people as well as to display my life and faith in front of many others."[64]

Schmidt took that calling very seriously and without any public fanfare. It was not an easy thing to do, either, because he was a tremendously private person who was never very comfortable around strangers. Unlike other Christian athletes who wore their faith on their sleeve, even imposing it on others, Schmidt was more reserved about his religious convictions. He displayed his faith in the community service work he did for others—especially underprivileged children—and he acknowledged his gratitude to God whenever his achievements were publicly recognized.

The year had been a blessing for Mike Schmidt, a reward for the struggles he endured earlier in his career. Time would tell whether Phillies fans had truly embraced him.

Chapter Five

$10 Million Man

The 1981 season was bittersweet for Mike Schmidt and the Phillies. Many baseball writers quickly wrote them off, considering their world championship of the previous year a fluke. "The Phillies won against all odds last year," wrote Steve Wulf of *Sports Illustrated*, who predicted a second-place finish, behind the Montreal Expos. In 1981, he contended, they were "headed for a breakdown." Wulf pointed out that key players like Larry Bowa and Tug McGraw were past their prime, though "the Phillies will probably need another year to convince themselves of that." Even Schmidt and Carlton "will be hard pressed to match their exceptional 1980 performances." Internal division between the players and their outspoken manager would also take its toll.[1] Despite the bleak forecast, the Phillies resumed their winning ways.

Schmidt enjoyed one of the best starts of his career. In April he cranked out a 13-game hitting streak and knocked in ten game-winning runs. By mid–June he was hitting .283 with 14 home runs, and the Phillies held a one and a half game lead over the second-place St. Louis Cardinals. Then, on June 12, the Players' Association called a strike.

Labor conflict had become as common to baseball as any other industry, the major issue being whether the owners or players should wield more control of the game. It hadn't always been that way. Prior to 1970 the reserve clause made a player the sole property of one team until the club decided to trade, release or retire him. It wasn't until 1966 that the Major League Players' Association secured better pension benefits, working conditions and a minimum salary through a formal labor contract with the owners. Known as the "Basic Agreement," the new arrangement significantly improved the bargaining position of the players. Three years later, in 1969, Curt Flood of the St. Louis Cardinals, who had been traded to the cellar-dwelling Phillies, refused to report to Philadelphia and filed a $3.1 million damage suit against his old team. In so doing, Flood challenged the reserve clause, taking his case all the way to the U.S. Supreme Court. On June 20, 1972, Justice Harry Blackmun agreed that the reserve clause was unfair, but stated that it was up to

Congress to change it. Flood's revolutionary action did, however, set the stage for the 1975 arbitration ruling that granted players the right to free agency that he sought.[2]

By the 1980s, players and owners jockeyed for advantage in the struggle for control. Both sides understood that baseball had always been a business, but now even the mask of innocence had yielded to money. In 1981, the issue was a new labor contract to replace the fourth basic agreement, which had expired on December 31, 1979. The owners were especially perturbed by the reentry draft concession they had made in the previous agreement because it undercut the reserve clause, freeing players to move to another team and, in many cases, making them multimillionaires. Some owners lost valuable players in the draft, only to be compensated with unproven, amateur prospects. Predictably, the owners sought to reverse this situation. They demanded that the reentry draft procedure be modified to force a club who signed a premier player to compensate the yielding club by relinquishing one of its top minor league prospects in return. In other words, the owners were demanding that the Players' Association surrender a concession that had been legally approved under the previous basic agreement. Marvin Miller, the players' negotiator, refused to concede to their demand.[3]

The players played without a contract throughout the 1980 season, acting on goodwill that an appointed committee of players and general managers would meet to study the reentry draft issue and that their recommendations would become part of the new basic agreement. When the committee failed to reach consensus by the assigned deadline of January 1, 1981, the owners imposed their own compensation plan and prepared for a strike. They paid Lloyds of London $2 million for $50 million in strike insurance, which guaranteed them $100,000 for each lost game over a six-week period in the event of a strike. The players, on the other hand, were placed at a great disadvantage. Their vote to strike in June destroyed whatever hopes they might have had to secure strike insurance, and a great majority stood to lose a considerable portion of their salaries.[4]

During the strike, Schmidt spent most of his time with his family, which had increased by one with the birth of a son, Jonathan. He was becoming an exceptional father who got up for early morning feedings, changed diapers and found ways to be involved with his two young children. He also took a weekend job at WCAU-TV in Philadelphia as a sports commentator. Inevitably, he generated controversy when, in his first commentary, he stated his belief that the players "earnestly tried to settle the dispute, voting to go on strike as a last resort," while the owners "went out and bought insurance." Immediately, the critics questioned his ability, as a high-salaried player, to offer objective commentary on the strike. Undaunted by the criticism, Schmidt continued to defend his views. "I'm not a baseball player when I'm doing the news," he explained. "I'm a newscaster, who has a responsibility to the public to address the hot issues. Nor did I say anything that wasn't factual. If an owner wants to comment on the facts, he's welcome to do so."[5]

Once started, the strike was fueled by a personal feud between Miller and the owners' representative Ray Grebey. By late July, as the strike threatened to end the 1981 season, Miller had gained the upper hand. He exploited the owners' fears by raising the possibility of the players' establishing their own league for the 1982 season. With fan hostility growing, their insurance policy with Lloyds about to expire and the possibility of lawsuits from individual players and organized umpires posing yet another threat, the profit-minded owners were forced to yield.[6]

The settlement called for the creation of a compensation pool that allowed each club to protect its best 24 players from the reentry draft. Those clubs not participating were permitted to protect 26 players. The arrangement benefited the players by allowing for the continuation of lucrative salary auctions for free agents. It also benefited the owners by allowing those clubs who lost a ranking free agent in the reentry draft to receive a major leaguer or a top minor leaguer in return. With the issue of compensation resolved, a new basic agreement was drafted and implemented.[7] Still, the strike tarnished baseball's image with the fans and cost both the players and owners significant revenue. The players forfeited an estimated $4 million a week in salaries, while the owners' losses totaled about $72 million.[8]

When the strike finally ended on July 31, 50 days of the season had been lost, and barely enough time remained for a credible resumption of play. Players were given one week to get back into playing condition. When play resumed on August 8, the Phillies seemed to lack the same punch they demonstrated earlier in the season, but Schmidt continued his torrid hitting. He was named the National League Player of the Month for August, compiling a .380 average, nine home runs and 24 RBI.

Because the Phils led the National League East when the strike occurred, they clinched a berth in postseason play. After losing the first two games of an intradivision playoff to Montreal, who had the best record after the resumption of play, the Phillies rallied to win the next two games. Unfortunately, Expos ace Steve Rogers ended their hopes for returning to the World Series with a 3–0, six-hit shut-out in the fifth and deciding game.[9] It was a disappointing ending to a season that many in the Phillies' front office believed would result in a second straight world championship. Significant changes would be made over the next few months.

Dallas Green had tired of managing the club. He was very critical of the team's mental approach to the game during the second half of the strike-shortened season. Among his chief targets was Schmidt, whom he criticized for skipping pregame infield practices. "I don't think he's as prepared for playing as he does," complained Green. "There's a pattern, like the throwing error in the early innings of a game. It would be better for the team if he took infield practice. If, in fact, he's a true leader, he's got to be out there. It might sound like surface stuff, but it ties in with being a super-class player."[10] In fact, Schmidt hadn't altered his pregame ritual at all from previous years. He would usually arrive at the ballpark around 3:00 P.M. for a 7:30 P.M. game. That gave him the time he needed to attend to his knees and whatever other aches he might have and to take batting practice. If he was in a slump, he would take extra BP, either in the batting cage beneath the stadium or out on the field. Because he believed third base to be a "reflex" position that depended primarily on instinctive reaction, Schmidt took only occasional infield practice. The only time he deviated from that routine was when the Phillies were playing on natural grass. Then he always took infield to familiarize himself with the playing surface, which was so different from the Astroturf at Veterans Stadium.[11]

Green was simply using Schmidt as a scapegoat for his own frustration over the Phils' inability to play to their potential. The more he cajoled them, the worse they seemed to play. He knew it, too. That is why Green wanted to return to the front office, this time as general manager. But Paul Owens was not ready to relinquish that post. Not surprisingly, when the Cubs offered him the GM's job in Chicago, Green took it.[12] The Phillies replaced him with Pat Corrales, a quiet but stern disciplinarian who had come up through the Phillies' organization as a catcher. Corrales, who had managed Texas to a third-place finish in 1979, was setting up a scouting system in Latin America for the Rangers when the Phillies offered him the job.[13]

Ruly Carpenter also left the organization, ending almost four decades of ownership by his family. Carpenter had tired of the demands of running a major league organization in the era of free agency. He refused to enter the bidding war, preferring to sign his homegrown talent to lucrative, long-term contracts. But he also realized that the future of the game rested with success in the free agent market and that, financially, he couldn't compete with some of the wealthier franchises. "It isn't fun anymore," he admitted. "In the past five years, 90 percent of my time has been spent on things not directly related to what happens on the field. Labor negotiations, negotiations on contracts, constant hassles with agents—the sideshows which have become more important than the game itself. During that time, it has become apparent to me that some deeply ingrained philosophical differences exist between the Carpenter family and some of the other owners as to how the baseball business should be conducted. It's come to the point where it is just impossible to continue with our philosophy. So, rather than continue to beat our heads against the wall, we have decided to sell."[14] On October 29, 1981, Carpenter sold the Phillies to a group of investors headed by Executive Vice President Bill Giles.[15]

For Giles, ownership of the Phillies was a dream come true. The son of former National League president Warren Giles, he was raised around the game. After college, he joined the front office of the Cincinnati Reds and, in 1962, moved on to Houston to become the publicity director for the new expansion Astros. Five years later he was promoted to vice president of the franchise. Giles joined the Phillies in 1969 as vice president in charge of business operations. His exceptional ability as a public relations director quickly allowed him to change the image of the Phillies from a ragtag band of losers to one of the more progressive winning teams in major league baseball. When Carpenter announced the sale of the team in March of 1981, Giles put together a group of investors and purchased the organization for $30 million. His partners included Taft Broadcasting Company, which owned Channel 29 in Philadelphia and had been granted broadcast rights to Phillies games for ten years beginning in 1982, and Fitz Eugene Dixon, former owner of the Philadelphia 76ers.[16]

One of the first priorities of the new owners was to sign Mike Schmidt, their franchise player, to a new, long-term contract. Schmidt was in the final year of a six-year, $700,000 contract in 1981. He had recently purchased a new home in suburban Media and hoped to retire as a Phillie. While the third baseman admitted that playing in New York or Los Angeles would have added "a lot more glitter" to his career, he felt "at peace with the city of Philadelphia, it's fans, and my life, in general."[17] Nevertheless, it would cost the Phillies a multiyear contract worth about $1.5 million a year to retain him. That was the going rate at the time for players of his caliber.

Mike Schmidt had emerged as the premier third baseman during an era that featured many stellar performers at the hot corner. He was joined in the National League by Ron Cey of the Dodgers, Bill Madlock of the Pirates and Bob Horner of the Braves. The American League could boast of George Brett of the Royals, Graig Nettles of the Yankees and Buddy Bell of the Rangers. While Nettles was the best at making great plays under pressure, and Brett and Madlock each hit for a higher average, Schmidt was widely considered by the baseball writers to be the best all-round third baseman in the game. He had a strong arm with a fairly quick and very accurate release. He had excellent reflexes that enabled him to react to hard-hit ground balls to his left and right. At the same time, Schmidt had the kind of fearlessness that characterized other great Hall of Fame third basemen like Pie Traynor, Eddie Mathews, and Brooks Robinson. He could take the liners and one-hops off his body, having a high threshold for pain.

In the strike-shortened season of 1981, Schmidt led the National League in homers (31), RBI (91), walks (73), runs scored (78), slugging average (.644) and on-base percentage (.435). He also compiled a career high .316 batting average, earned his sixth gold glove and won the All-Star Game for the National League with a 2-run homer off American League reliever Rollie Fingers. Not surprisingly, he received 21 of 24 first-place votes from the Baseball Writers who named him the National League MVP for the second straight year. With the distinction, Schmidt became just the ninth player in baseball history and the third in the National League to capture consecutive MVP Awards.[18]

Together with his power-hitting, which by 1982 resulted in 314 career home runs, Schmidt had established himself as a future Hall of Famer at the position. The Phillies realized that and knew they would have to meet his financial demands if they were to keep him in red and white pinstripes. Only a long-term, multi-million-dollar contract would allow him to complete his career in Philadelphia. In 1981, Schmidt would set the standard by which superstardom would be compensated.

The advent of free agency ushered in an era of escalating salaries. In 1970, only ten major leaguers earned more than $100,000. These were the biggest names in the sport, players like Hank Aaron, Frank Robinson, Roberto Clemente and Willie Mays. By the end of the decade, the average major league salary was $121,000, and several players had already passed the million-dollar mark, having signed multiyear contracts. Reggie Jackson had a five-year pact with the New York Yankees worth $2.93 million. Richie Zisk's contract with the Texas Rangers was worth $2.8 million over ten years. Jim Rice's seven-year deal with the Boston Red Sox averaged $770,000 a year. Dave Parker signed a five-year contract with the Pirates worth $900,000 a season. Only Nolan Ryan, however, enjoyed the distinction of having the first million-dollar annual salary, which he snared from the Houston Astros after rejecting an earlier, four-year offer of $3.56 million in 1979.[19]

Because their major priority was to field the best possible team, most of the owners contributed to escalating player salaries by entering the bidding war for free agents. At the same time, the owners attempted to manipulate the contracts of their better younger players to prevent them from becoming free agents once they reached their sixth year of service. Some owners responded to the dilemma by agreeing to long-term contracts. Typically, this would occur sometime after the player's fourth year of service, before he became eligible for free agency. If the contract was for, say, a five-year period, the owner would, in effect, buy out three years' worth of the player's free agency rights, retaining his services without having to pay the escalating rate for a premier player in the future.[20]

A multiyear contract also had its benefits for the player. No matter what might happen to him during the term of the contract, most, if not all, of the money would be guaranteed. Even if he were injured and his performance declined dramatically, his financial future was assured. Considering the wild rate of salary escalation during the 1980s, the only risk involved for the player in signing a long-term contract was that, should his performance improve dramatically, he would be locked in to a specific salary when his relative dollar value would be much higher.[21]

Schmidt was well aware of the politics surrounding salary negotiations. Surprisingly, he hired Arthur Rosenberg, an accountant and senior vice

Schmidt flashes a $10 million smile. Not only was he baseball's premier third baseman by 1982, having garnered back-to-back MVP Awards, but he was also the highest paid player in the National League. (*Courtesy of National Baseball Hall of Fame Library.*)

president with the brokerage firm of Dean Witter Reynolds, to be his agent. Rosenberg and Paul Shapiro, the attorney he hired to assist him, had no previous experience negotiating player salaries. The agent even admitted that "it took a lot of guts for Mike to go with me."[22] Schmidt disagreed. "Arthur and Paul had been talking about millions long before they walked into the negotiations," he said. "I wasn't dealing with rookies."[23]

Schmidt had met Rosenberg a few years earlier at a charity golf tournament. He was immediately attracted by the accountant's financial acumen and his modest demeanor. Rosenberg did not fit the mold of the fast-talking sports agent who took his cut and left. Schmidt's instincts were correct. The Phillies had offered him a contract in the range of $6 million for five years.[24] But Rosenberg knew he was worth much more.

He did his homework carefully, comparing Schmidt's statistical totals to the other high-salaried players in the game, calculating his worth in the current free agent market. He then approached Giles with a salary request "in the area of $1.7 million a year for six to eight years" with "the inclusion of a cost-of-living escalator clause," insisting that his client wanted a contract that would "let him retire as a Phillie."[25]

On December 22, the two sides agreed to a new, six-year deal worth $10 million, making Schmidt the highest paid player in National League history. Only Dave Winfield of the New York Yankees who had a $21 million, ten-year pact made more at the time.[26] Giles did secure a clause that would allow the Phillies to trade their star third baseman after three years if his knees would no longer allow him to play. "While Mike took a physical for purposes of insuring the contract, we wanted some way to get out of it after three years in case certain conditions arose," he explained. "It's a very complicated thing, but the machinery exists for a trade should he become a guy who, for instance, can still swing the bat but can't play third base for some reason."[27]

The Phillies were one of only a few clubs that could afford to make such a deal to retain their star player. The television revenue they would receive over the next decade made the transaction possible. But Giles had no illusions about having tighter control of his club's finances in negotiating subsequent player contracts because of it. "Schmidt is a special commodity," he admitted. "My philosophy is you have to take care of the key guys like Rose, Schmitty and Carlton. While you have to treat everybody fairly, we can't afford to lose one of those three players. Unfortunately, we're going to have to have tougher negotiations with some of the other players down the road or we just can't make it financially."[28]

At 32 years of age, Mike Schmidt was a multimillionaire. His financial security was guaranteed by playing a child's game. Was he worth $10 million? In the free market economy of major league baseball, where a player's performance was measured more by salary than statistics, he certainly deserved what he received. Considering the escalating salary structure of baseball in the 1980s, Schmidt probably could have earned even more had he played in a city like New York. There, players who had trouble hitting .250 demanded million-dollar salaries. If they didn't receive it, they would go to arbitration and win. There, owners billed the higher-salaried players as "superstars." Then, suddenly, they lost their passion to play the game and, having secured their wealth, went through the motions until they finally retired. Schmidt's work ethic would never allow for that kind of behavior.

"Fans are going to say, 'Let's see how he plays now, let's see if he tails off now,'" he predicted. "While I can't guarantee good years simply because you can't guarantee anything in baseball, I can handle that sort of pressure. I can tell you one thing: I'm going to be playing as hard as I've ever played and doing my best to improve. I'm not going to be satisfied with the level of the game I'm playing now. I'm going to try to get better, not because I make more money, but just because I have that kind of respect for the game."[29] His words would be prophetic. Years later, after he retired from the game, Schmidt could look back on his career with the satisfaction that he gave his best season after season. For the Phillies' third baseman, the significance of the strike-shortened season of 1981 had less to do with his statistical totals than with the financial security it afforded him and his family. To be sure, the strike prevented Schmidt from achieving two of the rarer feats in baseball. Not only had he come within 9 RBI of winning a triple crown in 1981, but had he not lost 50 games to the strike, the Phillies' slugger might have hit as many as 50 home runs, as well. Still, those records paled in comparison to the financial significance of the strike for him. "The labor dispute helped me tremendously as an individual," he admitted. "It allowed me to provide for my family, for my childrens' education, and that, in my estimation, is the most important thing I can do with my life."[30]

Chapter Six

Heroes, Bums and Boo-Birds

With the signing of a six-year, $10 million contract, Mike was committed to finishing his career in Philadelphia. Barring a trade, he would become a rarity for a sport in which hometown loyalty had been compromised by free agency. His decision to remain a Phillie, however, was puzzling, given the widespread criticism he suffered at the hands of the media and the fans. To say that Schmidt was "under appreciated" would be an understatement. While his power-hitting was greatly respected by the hometown fans, they, along with the press, often made him the scapegoat for the Phillies' misfortunes. Why, then, did Schmidt decide to remain in Philadelphia rather than declare free agency and move to another city where his talents would have been more appreciated?

"The overriding reason," he admitted, "is because Bill Giles made it financially worth my while to remain in Philadelphia. I was the highest paid player in baseball for a number of years and if not the highest paid, I was easily second or third. That was incentive enough to stay." Schmidt did not discount his wife's hometown roots or the desire to give his children a stable home life, both of which were major reasons to remain a Phillie.[1] But given the fickle treatment of the fans and the media, the financial reward seemed to be the determining factor in his decision. He would learn to live with the demanding baseball culture of the city. After all, history itself was against him.

Philadelphia's baseball fans have always enjoyed an infamous reputation. At best, they are "exceptionally demanding," at worst, "obnoxiously self-indulgent." It's part of an historical insecurity—an "underdog complex"—that can be traced back to the founding of the city in the late seventeenth century. Philadelphia's Quaker forefathers were considered troublesome outcasts in other colonies because they consciously disregarded all expressions of social class distinction. But in Philadelphia they found a home.[2] Their dissidence still remains an essential part of the urban culture. While Philadelphia may be a city of respected universities, nationally recognized museums, and an ever-diminishing coterie of blue bloods, its genuine spirit can be found in the clock-punchers and blue-collar workers, who define the city's character, especially when it comes to sports.

Although the fans have suffered an inglorious tradition of losing teams, there were memorable exceptions. An earlier era of winners set the precedent for the kind of ballplayer they adored. Connie Mack, the mythic manager of the Philadelphia Athletics, put together two championship dynasties, first from 1910 to 1914, and then, from 1929 to 1931. Those teams featured some of the most colorful personalities in the history of the game, including "Bucketfoot Al" Simmons, who would work himself into a homicidal rage before stepping up to the plate; George "Rube" Waddell, who chased fire trucks, loose women, and unruly fans; Robert "Lefty" Grove, who was known to lay waste to the clubhouse after losing a close game; and Mickey Cochrane, who hated to lose so much that he would stomp, scream and butt his head up against the dugout wall when it happened. The A's were sharp-witted and strong, reckless and carefree, brutally candid and shamelessly self-indulgent—much like the early twentieth century during which they played. They were also winners, compiling nine pennants and five world championships during their half-century in the City of Brotherly Love. In the process, the A's set a precedent for Philadelphia baseball as a "rough-and-tumble" game where you either "toughed it out" or "got out" of town.[3]

After the A's moved to Kansas City in 1954, Philadelphia's baseball fans were left with the Phillies. It must have been difficult to root for a team whose only successes came in 1915 and 1950, when they captured pennants. They were perennial losers who would receive the sympathy rather than the loyalty of a self-respecting fan in any other city. But in Philadelphia, they were alternately loved and vilified. Their most faithful followers were affectionately known as the "boo-birds." In fact, there are those players who actually believe that the home of the "boo," its very Cooperstown, is Philadelphia. If you're a Pete Rose or a Lenny Dykstra—a swaggering, trash-talking hustler who wears his emotions on his sleeve—Philadelphia is a wonderful place to play. Such throwbacks function in the same black-and-white world of heroes and bums as the fans. But God help the natural athlete who has a sensitive disposition, avoids controversy and seeks to be a role model, especially if he toils for a losing team! Such was Mike Schmidt's unenviable position in the eyes of the local media and fans. Predictably, the latter part of his career was by turns fulfilling and frustrating.

The 1982 Phillies had made some significant changes. Manager Pat Corrales, a soft-spoken contrast to Dallas Green, was quickly accepted by the players and began what would become one of the shortest tenures in Phillies history with much promise. Catcher Bob Boone, who had taken great criticism as spokesman in the player-owner struggle that resulted in the previous season's seven-week strike, was sold to the California Angels. Replacing him was Bo Diaz, who came over from the Cleveland Indians. Despite his reputation as a malingerer, Diaz's bat (.288 avg., 18 HR, 85 RBI) won over the hearts of the fans. The most heart-wrenching transition, however, came just after the end of the 1981 campaign when shortstop Larry Bowa was traded along with Ryne Sandberg to the Chicago Cubs for Ivan DeJesus. Not only did the Phillies lose a player who, in so many respects, was the heart of their team, but they threw in a future Hall of Famer, almost as an afterthought. It was one of the all-time worst trades in baseball history and DeJesus, who spent an unremarkable three years in Philadelphia, reinforced that fact by hitting a disappointing .239 in his first season with the Phils.[4]

Schmidt, who believed he was in the best physical condition of his career when he left for spring training, was ready for another MVP year. But only five games into the regular season he was sidelined with a severe injury. It happened on April 13, a raw, windy opening day at New York's Shea Stadium. During the top of the second inning, Schmidt lined a Randy Jones fastball into right field, a sure double. As he took off for first base, he felt a sharp stab in his back. It was so excruciating he doubled over in pain, holding his side. He had fractured a lower left rib with the force of his swing and, in the process, had torn the muscle away from his rib cage.[5]

Schmidt would be sidelined for weeks. It was two months before he could play without any pain. Without him, the Phillies got off to a poor start. When he returned to the lineup in late May they were barely playing .500 baseball and stuck in fourth place. Schmidt tried to make up for lost time. He pressed to hit the long ball, expecting more from himself than anyone, including the fans.[6] The more he pressed, the worse he performed. He entered the month of June with three homers and 13 RBIs. A month later his power-hitting totals modestly increased by four home runs and 11 RBIs, but he was hitting .300. "Maybe I ought to bat him lead-off," said Corrales, only half-jokingly realizing the seriousness of the rib injury. "Mike is a perfectionist. He wants to hit 40 homers, 120 RBIs and finish with a .300 average. That's the perfect baseball player. Now there's nothing wrong with that kind of thinking, but it does take its toll on a player—even of his caliber." Still, by mid–July, Corrales saw some signs that his premier power hitter was finally coming out of his funk.[7]

To be sure, Schmidt was beginning to drive the ball harder, but he had not completely healed from the injury, making it impossible for him to hit with the kind of power he had been accustomed to in previous seasons. The perfectionist in him refused to accept that fact. Amazingly, he still collected 33 homers and 80 RBIs by September and was hitting .300 on the mark.

In the opener of a critical three-game series against the division-leading

Cardinals, Schmidt hit a run-scoring single. The Phillies won that game, 2–0, behind the two-hit pitching of Steve Carlton and moved into first place by half a game. But they lost the next two and St. Louis regained first place by a one and a half game margin. A few weeks later, when the two teams met again in Philadelphia, Schmidt was mired in a 1-for-25 slump. Anticipating the Phillies' ultimate collapse, the media was unmerciful, blaming Schmidt for the team's misfortunes.[8]

Rose came to his friend's defense. "I don't think its fair to put the load on Mike's shoulders," he insisted. "When we've got guys not swinging the bat, he feels he has to get three hits and hit two out of the ballpark, and that puts too much pressure on him." He reminded the press that the Phillies' swoon was "a team effort" and that Schmidt can't be blamed if the rest of the team is slumping.[9] Rose was correct. Bo Diaz and Gary Matthews, the team's other two power hitters, were also struggling through their own slumps, but the press overlooked their struggles.

When asked about all the criticism, Schmidt responded with one of the most colorful remarks in Philadelphia sports history: "If we're going to start winning games, we'll have to break out of it offensively and play well. If we don't, then we don't deserve to be division champs. Two things are for sure, though—the sun is going to come up in the morning, and I'm not going to read the Philadelphia newspapers when it does. Only in Philadelphia can you experience the thrill of victory one night, and the agony of reading about it the next day."[10]

Schmidt never did break out of his slump, and the Cardinals went on to win the division with four games remaining in the season. The Phillies finished second, three games out with an 89–73 record. Schmidt's totals for the season were a .280 average, 87 RBIs and 35 home runs—good enough for third place in the National League home run races, behind Dave Kingman of the Mets and Dale Murphy of the Braves. It was a solid performance, especially considering the time he spent on the disabled list. But for the Phillies' slugger, it was a disappointing season: "If you base my performance on statistics, I've played the game in previous years at a level that is hard to match. When you set those kinds of standards for yourself, you also set them for the people who watch you. In that sense, I guess I was in a slump this year. But I look at what I achieved, the things I accomplished in only three good months and I can't help wondering what kind of numbers I could have produced if I had six good months."[11]

During the off season, the Phillies made some more personnel changes. In one of their more controversial moves, they acquired Von Hayes (a much heralded prospect in the Cleveland organization) for Manny Trillo (who wanted a long-term contract), outfielder George Vukovich, shortstop Julio Franco and two minor league prospects. The "five-for-one" deal was initially hailed as a good one. Hayes, a young left-handed hitter, was being compared to both Ted Williams and Stan Musial by the baseball experts. But over the course of his nine-year career with the Phillies, he proved to be a disappointment.[12] Pitcher Mike Krukow was traded to San Francisco for second baseman Joe Morgan and reliever Al Holland. Power-hitting first baseman Tony Pérez was also signed after his unconditional release from Boston.[13] Along with Pete Rose, Pérez and Morgan gave the Phillies three members of the once-powerful Big Red Machine and the kind of experience necessary to capture another pennant. It also gave the team a rather elderly complexion, as 22 of the players on the 40-man roster were over 30 years of age. Among the "most seasoned" veterans were Rose (41), Pérez and pitcher Ron Reed (40), Morgan and outfielder Bill Robinson (39), and pitchers Steve Carlton and Tug McGraw (38). Collectively, the 1983 Phillies were more affectionately known as the "Wheeze Kids," an appropriate moniker considering that the 1950 pennant winners were called the "Whiz Kids" and that 1983 marked the centennial anniversary of the Phillies organization.[14]

Regardless of the age issue, there was good reason to acquire Morgan and Pérez. Having traded away Trillo, the Phillies needed an experienced second baseman that could mentor their younger prospect, Juan Samuel. Morgan, who helped to make the Astros and Giants contenders after leaving Cincinnati, was a perfect solution to the dilemma. The Phillies also needed a right-handed pinch hitter with some clout and a player who could spell Rose at first base. Not only was Rose the oldest player on the team, but his .271 average of the previous year raised questions about his ability to play on a regular basis. Pérez, who helped to make contenders out of the Montreal Expos and the Red Sox after leaving the Reds, fit nicely into the Phils' plans. Between the three of them, Rose, Morgan and Pérez brought an amazing wealth of knowledge and experience to the Phillies, having played in a total of 7,925 games, collecting 8,711 hits, scoring 4,729 runs and sporting seven World Series championship rings.[15]

Luck also played a significant role in the Phillies' hopes for another pennant in 1983. The National League East was an embarrassment that season. No one took command through the first half of the season, and yet the Phillies found themselves in first place at the All-Star break. Several key Phillies were struggling. Rose was laboring at the plate and in the field and, as a result, was being platooned with rookie Len Matuszak. Matthews, who had 17 game-winning RBIs the previous season, had only three. And Morgan was hitting an anemic .201, splitting second base duties with rookie Juan Samuel.[16] In fact, there wasn't a consistent bat in the lineup. But Schmidt suffered the worst slump.

Entering May, the Phillies' slugger was hitting .353 with seven homers and 23 RBIs. Over the next month he was 7-for-66, his average slipping to .245. The nadir of his 19-game slump came on May 27 in a game against the Montreal Expos. Schmidt went 0-for-4, fouling out his first time up, then striking out on his next three plate appearances. The following night he struck out on three pitches in each of his first four at-bats. Finally, in his fifth at-bat, he hit the first pitch for a game-winning home run.[17]

Owens, disappointed with his team's mediocre play, fired Corrales and assumed the duties of field manager once again. The Phils responded by winning 11 in a row, and 14 of their next 16 games. Owens constantly juggled the lineup, looking for the right offensive combination. Through it all, the media ignored the poor hitting of Diaz, Matthews, Morgan and Hayes and focused their criticism on Schmidt, who was flirting with the .240 mark for most of the season. Peter Pascarelli of the *Philadelphia Inquirer* seemed to take special pleasure in criticizing him for "leaving more runners on base than anyone else in the lineup" and complaining that Schmidt's power production "comes in small stretches around long droughts." Pascarelli also projected that Schmidt's "strikeout total will be 150 for the year" and suggested that if Mike didn't "put together four explosive weeks" down the stretch, it would be his fault that the Phillies had underachieved.[18]

After one especially vicious personal attack, Schmidt felt as if he had "just hit a brick wall with the media in terms of trust and respect." He considered joining Steve Carlton in taking an unconditional vow of silence when it came to the press, but decided against it, realizing that such criticism was part of the price he had to pay for being successful. Instead, he continued to be one of the most cooperative and approachable professional athletes in the city. "When you're up at the top, there are so many people who want to take shots at you," he said. "Being a professional athlete though, means you're in the public eye and you get paid well. You have to realize that success breeds jealousy. Besides, nobody boos or gives bad press to a mediocre player, only the best ones get it."[19]

Schmidt was human, though, and all the criticism and lineup juggling had taken its toll on him. On September 9, he lashed out against the Phillies' management. "We have no sense of direction," he complained. "Nobody is sure who the manager is around here. As a veteran player, I'm disappointed in the way the front office has handled this season. We've got a team full of guys who are capable of turning on a switch, but two weeks later, you wouldn't know it was the same club if you looked at the lineup. What we've got is an organization full of soap opera problems."[20] It was an uncharacteristic outburst from a player who usually went about his business avoiding distractions and controversies. Predictably, Owens was quick to reply. "Schmidt's problem is that he thinks too much. He should just go out and play the game, using the ability God gave him."[21] Nevertheless, Schmidt's teammates appreciated his words, believing that only he, as the undisputed team leader, could register their dissatisfaction with management.

When all the controversy finally died down, the Phillies found themselves in first place. The Expos, who had been favored to win the division, self-destructed down the stretch. St. Louis, also considered a better team than the Phillies, choked in mid-season and never regrouped. The Phils took advantage of their rivals' misfortunes and clinched the division on September 28 with a 2–0 victory over the Chicago Cubs at Wrigley Field.[22]

The Phils faced the Dodgers in the playoffs with the series opening in Los Angeles on October 4. Jerry Reuss faced Steve Carlton, who had just notched his three hundredth career victory a month earlier. Schmidt hit a solo homer in the first inning and Lefty pitched seven and a half masterful innings with Holland coming in to close the 1–0 victory. The Dodgers evened the series the following day with a 4–1 win behind the pitching of Fernando Valenzuela. Gary Matthews' solo homer in the second accounted for the only Phillie run. The playoffs resumed in Philadelphia on Friday night, October 7. Rookie Charles Hudson faced Bob Welch of the Dodgers and pitched a complete game victory, 7–2. Though Dodger outfielder Mike Marshall hit a two-run homer in the fourth, Hudson allowed just three other hits and struck out nine. Gary Matthews proved to be a one-man wrecking crew, clubbing a solo homer in the fourth, a two-run single in the fifth, and another run-scoring base hit in the seventh. Carlton returned to the mound for the pennant clincher the following day. Although Lefty had to leave the game with a sore back after the sixth inning, he enjoyed a 7–1 lead at the time, largely due to a three-run homer by Matthews, who was later named the MVP of the series.[23] Schmidt went 7-for-15 in the playoffs for a .467 average with two doubles, a homer and two RBIs. His World Series against the Baltimore Orioles would be much less productive.

The Orioles were slight favorites to win the Series, having captured the American League East by six games and then quickly dispatching the Chicago White Sox in the league championship series, three games to one. Managed by first-year skipper Joe Altobelli, Baltimore had an outstanding pitching staff, featuring left-handers Scott McGregor (18–7) and Mike Flanagan (12–4), rookie right-handers Mike Boddicker (16–8) and Storm Davis (13–7), and closer Tippy Martinez (9–3, 21 saves). The Birds also enjoyed a potent offense that centered around Cal Ripken, a 23-year-old shortstop who was also the League MVP (.318 avg., 27 HR, 102 RBI), and veteran first baseman Eddie Murray (.306 avg., 33 HR, 111 RBI). The Orioles could also boast of an excellent defensive catcher in Rick Dempsey and an effective outfield platoon of six players who could all hit well.[24]

Game One was played October 11, a rainy Friday evening in Baltimore. Phillies ace John Denny, the National League Cy Young Award winner, faced the Orioles' Scott McGregor in a classic pitcher's duel. Solo homers by Joe Morgan and Garry Maddox gave the Phils a 2–1 win.[25] The next day Baltimore rode a dazzling three-hitter by Mike Boddicker for a 4–1 win, evening the Series.[26]

Interestingly, the bats of both clubs' premier power hitters fell silent through the first two games. Eddie Murray of the Orioles suffered through a 1-for-8 performance, while Schmidt found himself in an 0-for-8 slump. When Murray was asked about the coincidence and whether it bothered him, he replied, "I've been going through it all my life. I think Mike Schmidt is going through the same thing. The media keeps bringing it up. So its difficult to ignore." As Murray spoke, he became more agitated by the question. "What do you expect?" he snapped. "We're out there doing the best we can and if we don't deliver, you jump in our faces. How would you like it?"[27]

Game Three was another pitcher's duel, this one between two southpaws, Steve Carlton and Mike Flanagan. But the game is probably better remembered for Owens' controversial decision to bench Pete Rose in favor of Tony Pérez at first base. "I've got to do something to get more offense," the Phillies' manager explained. "We've gotten only eight hits in two days. Besides, I've got a good feeling about Tony."[28] While Rose was only 1-for-8 in the first two games of the Series, he hit .283 against left-handers during the regular season, whereas Pérez hit only .205. Benching a player with Rose's postseason experience was a panic move at a time when, with the series tied at one game apiece, there was no reason to panic. "It's just not the way baseball is played," Rose told Howard Cosell in a postgame interview. "Here we are, the third game of the World Series, and probably the two most surprised guys in this ballpark were myself and Tony Pérez. It's just embarrassing."[29]

On the field, the game was decided by a Rick Dempsey double and a run-scoring single by Benny Ayala in the seventh inning. Unfortunately, the Phils were on the losing end once again, 3–2.[30]

By Game Four Schmidt was riding an 0-for-12 slump. John Denny faced Storm Davis in a scoreless pitcher's duel until the fourth inning when Baltimore loaded the bases on consecutive singles by Jim Dwyer, Cal Ripken and Eddie Murray. After fanning John Lowenstein, Denny surrendered a two-run single to Rich Dauer. The Phillies came back in the bottom of the inning. Rose singled and Schmidt followed with a broken-bat pop fly that fell into short left-center. It would be his only hit of the Series. Joe Lefebvre then doubled, cutting the score to 2–1. Philadelphia took the lead in the fifth on doubles by Bo Diaz and Pete Rose and a single by Denny, but the O's regained the lead in the sixth, 4–3, and added a fifth run in the seventh. Schmidt had another opportunity to redeem himself in the eighth. Down by two runs with Rose on first base, the Phillies were hoping that their slugger had finally broken out of his funk. Orioles reliever Sammy Stewart threw him a cut fastball out over the plate and Schmidt, trying to tie the game up with one swing, hit a pop foul down the third base line to end the inning. The boo-birds let loose on him as he returned to the dugout. "That was the first time they booed me in the Series," he noted afterward. "They put up with me making outs as much as they could and I can understand that. I'm just as disappointed as they are. They're not making it tough on me. I guess I'm making it tough for myself to hit."[31] The Phils fell short by a run in the ninth and lost a heart-breaker, 5–4.

Baltimore clinched the championship the following evening with a 5–0 romp of the Phils. Scott McGregor yielded just five base hits and Eddie Murray broke out of his slump with two homers. Schmidt, on the other hand, never got started. He went 1-for-20 with six strikeouts in the Series. Orioles pitchers kept teasing him with high fastballs, and he kept pressing harder and harder to hit them.[32]

Three days after the Series had ended, Pete Rose was released. The first baseman's .245 average and the prospect of paying another one million dollars for a man who would become a part-time player convinced Bill Giles to sever the relationship. While Rose accepted his unconditional release with his characteristic homespun philosophy, he made it clear that he intended to play elsewhere on an everyday basis. "If its the best thing for me, then I'll hit the road," said the 42-year-old baseball legend. "I don't like to play part-time. I've been an everyday player for so many years it's hard for me to play three days a week. I'm sure there are some teams out there who want me."[33] There were. The Montreal Expos quickly signed Rose, making him a regular in their lineup. Perhaps the most fitting epitaph to the Rose era came from Schmidt, who said, "The Phillies had gone a long, long time without being in a World Series, until Pete Rose arrived. Pete's been in two of them here. He's also been a great friend of mine. I've accomplished a lot during his time here, and I think a great deal of that success has to do with him." While the third baseman hated to see his best friend go, he realized that "time marches on. So do careers as well as life itself and you can't ignore that. I'll be in the same boat some day. God willing, it will be four or five years down the road, but I'll be in the same boat, too." Schmidt chuckled, thinking about his dismal 1-for-20 World Series. "Probably a lot of guys wish I were in that same boat right now," he added.[34]

Morgan and Pérez were also released. Owens was desperately trying to avoid the kind of collapse the Cincinnati Reds experienced in the late 1970s after their big names moved on. His plan was to stay competitive by retaining the team's most talented players like Schmidt and Carlton, while phasing in younger prospects. At 36 years of age, the Phillies' slugger found himself as one of the most seasoned veterans on the team, and one the younger players turned to increasingly for leadership.

Schmidt wasn't the same kind of team leader as Rose, though. Nor did he pretend to be. "Pete lived baseball 24 hours a day," he said. "That's great, but it's not me. I have other interests. I have a family. I'm a father. I dedicate myself to baseball totally once the season starts. But there's more to my life than baseball."[35]

One of the leadership roles Schmidt took very seriously was becoming a role model for youngsters. His active involvement as a fund-raiser for such organizations as the United Way, the Philadelphia Child Guidance Clinic, and the Christian Children's Fund set an example for other athletes, who watched him give something back to the community by renewing the implicit commitment a professional athlete makes as a hero to kids. Being a dedicated and caring parent also compelled him to be a role model for other children. He lamented the fact that "grade school kids are experiencing now what I didn't experience until college. If a kid in the eighth grade has run the gamut of experiences from sex to drugs to liquor, if he's gotten in the habit of altering his state of mind as often as he can, is he going to grow out of it by the time he's 20?"

Schmidt realized that the temptations of youth were enhanced by a society that largely ignored traditional family values. Peer pressure only added to the quest for immediate gratification without considering the long-term consequences. "When I was growing up, I followed the crowd," he admitted. "That's why it bothers me to go to schools today and see that there's no respect for hygiene, no respect for the way you look, no respect for teachers, no respect for the mind. There's only respect for whoever has the most fun."[36]

Schmidt's Christian faith only served to strengthen his commitment to young people by reminding him of his obligations to other human beings. "The Lord has a plan for each one of us and His plan for my life has been a wonderful plan," he said. "I believe that my obligation for the many blessings He has given me is to live my life as an example for children. If I can affect those lives in a positive way, whether it's something I say, or something I do, or something I give, or just living my life as an example so people can say, 'This guy's a good guy, a family man, who knows how to love, how to care for people, how to be humble,' then I believe I have lived up to my responsibility."[37]

Schmidt's example was a refreshing one during an era when most professional athletes discouraged youngsters from considering them as heroes. He worked hard at being a good role model for kids, and it wasn't always easy. During the winter of 1983, after his disappointing World Series performance, he was tracking his five-year-old daughter's school bus in a snowstorm. She had forgotten her lunch and he was trying to catch up with her. When he flagged down another bus to inquire about his daughter's route, some junior high boys recognized him and began yelling, "That's Mike Schmidt! That's Mike Schmidt!" Then, from the back of the bus, one youngster shouted, "Choker!" It hurt him deeply.[38]

An introverted person by nature, Schmidt had difficulty understanding the mentality of the Phillies' most vocal fans. "You're trying your damnedest," he once admitted. "You strike out and they boo you. I act like it doesn't bother me, like I don't hear anything the fans say, but the truth is I hear every word of it and it kills me. I know people say booing shouldn't bother a veteran but they must be talking about a 'veteran robot.' Players are human beings, and some are more sensitive than others. I guess if I were the kind of player who could go out on the field every day with a carefree attitude, without putting a lot of pressure on myself, I wouldn't mind all the booing. But I take it all too seriously. I also take failure too harshly. If I didn't, I wouldn't care and then maybe I would have never succeeded at this game. It's a catch–22 thing."[39]

While Schmidt probably could have accepted the booing, it was the fickle treatment of so many fans that frustrated him the most. It was as if they were toying with his emotions, booing him one moment and giving him a standing ovation the next. A classic example occurred on Opening Day 1984 at the Vet against the Houston Astros. For seven and a half innings Schmidt was booed unmercifully. Having to face Nolan Ryan didn't contribute much to his cause. He struck out once, popped up twice, stranding a total of six runners. To add insult to injury, the third baseman couldn't catch up to a Craig Reynolds pop foul down the foul line in the top of the eighth, giving the Astros' shortstop new life at the plate. When he hit the next pitch into the stands for a 1–0 Houston lead, the fans showered Schmidt with a barrage of jeers. Then, in the bottom of the inning, Schmidt hit a three-run homer, giving the Phillies a 3–1 victory. As he rounded the bases, the crowd of 37,236 went wild cheering him.[40]

Bill Giles tried to explain the fans' treatment of Schmidt in terms of the relationship between a father and a son, insisting that the boos were "not because they didn't like Schmidt, but because they expected more of him." But the Phillies' president had to concede that his franchise player was "not as popular as he should be in Philadelphia" and that "was a shame."[41]

Why Schmidt was the most relentlessly booed athlete in Philadelphia sports history can be attributed to three factors. First, he was a naturally gifted athlete who had an impressive physical appearance. Although Schmidt worked hard to improve his performance, the physical aspect of the game came more easily to him than to others. He had the raw power and exceptional coordination to hit a baseball for distance. His broad shoulders and muscular body allowed him to excel at the physical aspects of the game and stand out in a sport that had never been distinguished by exceptional-looking physical specimens. In fact, Pete Rose jokingly coveted Schmidt's physique so much that he offered to trade his own body as well as his wife's and throw in some cash besides to acquire it![42] Schmidt was labeled a "natural" in terms of his God-given talent and appearance, and that didn't play well in Philly.

Second, and related to his exceptional athletic ability, was the "Mr. Cool" image Schmidt unconsciously projected. Fans often scorned him as baseball's ultimate ice man because he gave the impression that he was strutting whenever he jogged to first base after a walk or returned to the dugout after the end of an inning. For them, it was appropriate to strut around the bases after hitting a home run, in fact, it was desirable, almost as if to spite the opposing team, something any Philadelphia fan would relish. But at any other time, "strutting" meant you had an "attitude." Together with his extraordinary ability to play the game, Schmidt's "cool" demeanor was interpreted by the fans as "ego-centric" and "uncaring." The fans wanted him to emote when things didn't go his way, to get sweaty and dirty, to throw his batting helmet after a strike-out, to get tossed out of the game when he disagreed with a call. Instead, Schmidt rarely challenged an umpire's decision. After striking out, he would simply return to the dugout, thinking about how he could get a hit the next time up. He understood that his inability to show emotion on the field annoyed the fans, admitting that he "often wished [he] didn't have the 'Mr. Cool' label." But he found it necessary to "remain as calm and collected as possi-ble under all circumstances, whether it be striking out with the bases loaded or hitting a grand slam home run." Such reservedness, he believed, was "needed to succeed at the game."[43]

Finally, there was the issue of his multimillion-dollar salary. Because Schmidt's ascendancy as one of the premier power hitters in the game coin-cided with a period of wild escalation of salaries, he was paid top dollar. In fact, he was instrumental in establishing the "going rate" for superstars in 1981 with his $10 million contract. Fans were jealous of his affluence, espe-cially when he did not meet their expectations of behavioral conduct on the field. Inevitably, the salary issue was raised whenever he experienced a slump or registered his frustration with the fans in the newspapers.

These three factors made Schmidt's relationship with the Philadelphia fans a no-win situation. No matter how hard he tried to win over their alle-giance, he always seemed to fall short. By the mid–1980s, however, he did learn how to handle the fickle treatment of the fans more constructively than he had in the past. While he continued to speak his mind to the press, Schmidt also learned to show more emotion on the field and to do so in a positive way that would not compromise his integrity. His headfirst leap onto a pile of teammates after the final out of the 1980 World Series, for example, is indeli-bly etched in the minds of many Philadelphians and is still one of the most treasured images in the city's sports history. Other, less dramatic moments occurred as well. In one game, Schmidt, in pursuit of a foul pop-up down the left-field line, reached into a box seat to make the catch. Not only did he snag the ball, but also a fan's hat in the process. The Phillies' third baseman cer-emoniously carried his glove—with the ball and the fan's hat—over to the umpire who proceeded to call the batter out. The fans went crazy because it was an amusing sight that played to their emotions.[44]

Schmidt also learned to appreciate the humorous side of all the criticism. On one occasion, when he was struggling through an especially bad slump, a boo-bird regular jeered him relentlessly. Every time the Phillies' slugger stepped up to the plate, the irascible fan would holler, "Hey Schmidt, you better earn that million dollars!" Instead of dwelling on the negative, Schmidt admitted that he was actually "tempted to step out of the batter's box, walk over to the fence, and say to him, very softly, 'That's two million.'"[45]

What's more, Schmidt learned to laugh at himself once in a while. One of the most memorable incidents came in 1985 when he briefly switched positions to first base. Known as the "wig and sunglasses prank," it began when Schmidt gave an interview to Peter Hadekel of the *Montreal Gazette* in mid–April. Frustrated by a particularly abusive reception from the fans a few nights before, Schmidt described the hometown faithful as "beyond help" and "a mob scene." "Whatever I've got in my career now, I would have had a great deal more if I'd played in Los Angeles or Chicago," he said. "You name a town—a place where the fans were just grateful to have me around."[46]

As usual, the Phillies' star was direct. His words were tinged with frustration, disappointment, and bitterness. It was a mistake. Although he had a right to his feelings, Schmidt should not have aired them in a public arena. He only served to alienate himself from the fans and the press, which was only too willing to capitalize on his mistake.

Two months later, on June 29, the interview was published in the *Gazette*. The next day, Schmidt's remarks made the headlines in Philadelphia. After confirming that he did, in fact, give the interview, the Phillies' slugger admitted that he "regretted saying what I said" and clarified his position. He pointed out that the interview had been done much earlier in the season, when the Phillies were "suffering through a miserable stretch" and the fans "were not sure which way to go." He then softened many of his criticisms. "I know that I am a little too sensitive," he admitted. "But I do get disappointed with the behavior of Phillies fans when my performance is sub par. How soon they forget some of the good things that have happened. It's easy to play when you're in first place and it's easy to be a fan when your team is winning every day. But every team and every player is going to have their peaks and valleys. Philadelphia is the toughest town I've been around when you're in a valley." Offering a truce, Schmidt added that he "hoped the fans don't feel that I'm proud of my .237 batting average. I feel worse about my performance this season than any of the fans. But I can't quit. I've got to keep going out there every day to get out of the slump."[47]

Despite his controversial remarks, Schmidt dismissed the suggestion that he sounded as if he wanted to be traded. "I never want to be traded," he insisted. "I love my home, my kids are in school and they love the Philadelphia area. I also have friends in town as well as business interests. Our roots are here."[48]

When the Phillies returned home from Montreal on July 1, Schmidt braced himself for the ultimate boo-bird reception. During the introductions preceding the Phils' game with the Cubs, the fans prepared to give Schmidt a greeting he would never forget. The hostility against the Phillies' superstar was so thick you could feel it in the air. Then, suddenly, a bewigged figure wearing a pair of dark sunglasses trotted out onto the field to take his position at first base. The physique belonged to Mike Schmidt, so did the uniform number. But nobody could make out the face, which was hidden under a mass of dark brown dreadlocks. For a split second, the fans didn't know what to do. Was it actually Schmidt incognito? Had "Mr. Cool" lost his mind, or had he finally learned not to take himself so seriously?

Regardless of fan opinion, Schmidt was delivering a psychological master stroke. He had defused a potentially embarrassing situation by borrowing the props from clubhouse clown and teammate Larry Anderson. His self-deprecating sense of humor had saved the day. After a few seconds of uncertainty, the fans took to their feet, responding with a boisterous round of applause. No self-respecting boo-bird, even in his wildest of dreams, could have predicted that Schmidt would get himself a standing ovation that day. More important, the incident marked the beginning of a new, more appreciative relationship between the Phillies' slugger and the fans. Of course, they would continue to boo him in the future, but they did it with a certain degree of respect.[49]

After harshly criticizing Phillies fans in a 1985 Montreal newspaper interview, Schmidt donned a wig and sunglasses and took the field incognito. It was the beginning of a truce between the sometimes too sensitive slugger and Philadelphia's exceptionally demanding fans. (*Courtesy of AP/Wide World Photos.*)

Schmidt also learned to put his relationship with the fans in a better perspective. Whenever the booing started, he'd check himself by remembering the truly important things in his life. "I'm standing there getting showered with boos, but it doesn't seem to bother me as much anymore," he said. "Instead, I consider it a test that God believes will be good for me and I'm grateful for the more important things He's given me in life. I've got two healthy kids, a loving wife, healthy parents. I've got all the things in life that are really important. So I just try to keep all those things in a proper perspective and draw strength from that."[50]

Schmidt would need to keep a healthy perspective on life, because the Phillies struggled after 1983. The following season, the team dropped to fourth place, barely playing .500 baseball. And 1985 was worse. The Phils lost 34 of their first 52 games and never came close to contending in a year when they were expected to run away with their division. Instead, they finished a dismal fifth, 26 games out.[51] Owens' plan to remain competitive by fielding a mixture of proven stars, seasoned veterans and young prospects simply didn't pan out. The Phillies' clubhouse became a revolving door during those years, a futile attempt to discover a winning combination.

After a poor start in 1985, the Phillies attempted to revive the season by asking Schmidt to move to first base to make room for infield prospect Rick Schu. By late May, the Phils' slugger was hitting an anemic .189 and had a disappointing total of five home runs and 15 RBIs. Schu, on the other hand, was putting up impressive numbers at Triple A Portland, compiling a .284 average with four homers and 22 RBIs in 41 games. He looked as if he could contribute some punch to a faltering lineup.[52]

"I'm nervous about moving to first base," said Schmidt, who reluctantly agreed to the move. "But if this is what the club wants me to do and if this is what they feel will help, then I'll do it." At the same time he couldn't help but question the move. "The timing is sort of funny," he wondered aloud. "While we're ten games below .500 and I haven't been performing well defensively, I can't see myself being anything more than adequate for a while. So, I'm not quite sure how bringing up an inexperienced right-handed hitter will help. It just might weaken us at two positions. Having said that, I also understand that a lot of people in the organization think Schu is going to be a heck of a player. If he can do the job at third, then maybe I'll play at first for the next three to four years. We'll just have to see."[53] Schu was not as concerned: "I'm ready, I've worked hard to get back to the big club, and I'm looking forward to playing. Replacing Mike at third puts some added pressure on me, I guess. But it's not like he'll be out of the lineup. All I can do is just play hard like I always did. I feel comfortable playing third base, and I've been swinging the bat pretty well the last few weeks, so I can't wait to get started."[54]

While the move did raise some eyebrows, there was some logic to it. Defensively, Schmidt was not performing as well as he had in the past. He had already made nine errors that season and was well on his way to matching the 26 he committed the previous year. The brain trust was beginning to wonder if the wear and tear of playing third had taken its toll on their 36-year-old franchise player. His knees had always been questionable. He had to ice them after every game. But recently, he was suffering from an assortment of leg injuries. At the time of the switch he was trying to play with a sore ankle as well as a hamstring pull, which limited his range at the hot corner. Schu, on the other hand, was only 23. He had exceptional range in the field and a better arm than Schmidt, as well as a strong bat. Additionally, the move would solve the ongoing problem the Phillies were having finding a first baseman.

John Russell, a power-hitting outfield prospect, had been promoted to learn the position earlier in the season. But he was hitting a disappointing .209 and never gained much confidence at the position. Nor did the alternative of platooning veteran utility men Tim Corcoran and John Wockenfuss work out. Neither could give the team the kind of offensive production it needed. While Schmidt wouldn't be any worse than Russell at first, his bat was clearly better than all three players. Moreover, his athletic ability would, in time, make him into more than an "adequate" first baseman.[55] As it turned out, the switch to first allowed Mike to reconsider his hitting style, paving the way for his third MVP season in 1986.

Having to learn a new position took some of the pressure off him at the plate. When he took batting practice, he began to pay closer attention to his swing. Then, on August 15, in a game against Dwight Gooden and the Mets at Shea Stadium, it all fell into place. During pregame batting practice, he made a conscious effort to drive the ball downward with every swing. He noticed that the ball jumped off his bat with much more authority than it had before. Later, in his first at-bat, Schmidt swung downward on a Gooden fastball and hit an RBI single up the middle. In his next plate appearance, he hit a three-run homer off the scoreboard in right center, using the same downward swing. "I've carried those at-bats with me ever since," he said, crediting the downswing for his success. "I finally realized that I wasn't driving through the ball, I was hitting up on it. I went back to driving it down and waiting on the pitch. The walk is my barometer. When I'm going good, I get one or two walks a game. But I was chasing pitches out of the strike zone earlier this season. I began to chase high pitches, and didn't want to hit my own pitch. Now that I use the downswing, more of my swings result in contact as opposed to foul balls. My strikeouts have gone down and my RBIs and walks have gone up."[56] By September 1, Schmidt's hitting had improved dramatically. He had hit 23 homers, collected 63 RBIs and could boast of a .321 average. By season's end he was among the league leaders in homers (33) and RBI (93).

Schmidt's momentum carried over into the 1986 campaign, a season in which he recaptured the home run and RBI crowns. More impressively, the change in his approach to hitting allowed him to secure his third MVP Award. Unfortunately, the Phillies finished a distant second, 21 and a half games behind the Mets, who went on to capture the World Series that year.

The Phils' unremarkable finish raised the recurring question: Should the MVP go to a member of a championship team (or at least a strong contender), or to the player enjoying the greatest individual success? Schmidt's numbers—.290 average, 37 HR, 119 RBI, .547 slugging percentage—were convincing enough for the Baseball Writers, who made Schmidt a landslide winner, giving him 15 of 24 first-place votes. Glenn Davis of the National League West champion Houston Astros and Gary Carter of the Mets finished a distant second and third, respectively. While Carter believed that the award "should have gone to a member of the [world champion] Mets," his teammate Keith Hernandez, who was also in the running for the award, insisted that he "wasn't disappointed at all" with the Writers' choice of Schmidt. "I'd have voted for Mike Schmidt, too," he insisted. "He put up great numbers and is deserving. He was the most valuable player this year. No player on the winning teams stood out with great statistical years. Anybody else besides Schmidt who thought they had a chance was only fooling themselves."[57]

Having garnered his third MVP, the Phillies' superstar was in an exclusive class of players. Stan Musial of the St. Louis Cardinals and Roy Campanella of the Brooklyn Dodgers were the only other National Leaguers to have received the award three times before. Only four American Leaguers shared that honor: Jimmie Foxx of the Philadelphia Athletics, and Joe DiMaggio, Yogi Berra and Mickey Mantle, all of whom played for the Yankees. Clearly, Schmidt had solidified his Hall of Fame credentials with the achievement. But quite apart from that illustrious company, this MVP held special meaning for him. At an age when most players are forced to consider retirement, Schmidt proved that he could reinvent himself, remaining at the top of his game. All he had to do was look around the clubhouse to realize that, in time, a major leaguer had to come to terms with his own mortality. Earlier in the season, his best friend, Garry Maddox, retired after wrestling with a series of nagging back problems. Another close friend, Steve Carlton, was given his release, having lost his ability to win consistently. Yet here was Schmidt, at the age of 37, returning to third base, capturing his tenth Gold Glove and winning a third MVP.

"Since my last MVP in 1981, there have been some valleys," he admitted when asked about his extraordinary achievement. "I had some good years and some so-so years. There were some hard times. People were questioning whether I could still cut it at third base. And there was some talk that it was time to trade Mike Schmidt. So to rebound to this level at the age of 37 is quite gratifying. Because the end of my career is near, there is much more pressure to do well, to go out on top. For both of those reasons, this is a very special thing for me."[58]

Finally, as he had done so often before, Schmidt "thank[ed] God for the desire to excel as a professional athlete."[59] It was his way of witnessing his faith without imposing it on others. That is not to say that he downplayed the significance of his faith. In fact, Schmidt believed that all the national publicity he was given for his on-field accomplishments in 1986 only served to bring more attention to his relationship with God. "Right now," he admitted, "I consider myself one of His many useful people. My faith doesn't make me better than anyone else, it just gives me the power to cope with life as well as the will to player harder. I understand that whatever happens in my life is God's will. I guess that's why I am a thoroughly happy man and only a small part of that has to do with baseball and the good season I've had."[60]

Heroes, bums and boo-birds. Mike Schmidt had experienced it all during his years of "peaks and valleys" with the Phillies. Sometimes the frustration and pain caused him to speak out against management or the fans. At other times, he simply went about his business. In the process, he had become the greatest third baseman in the history of the game.

Chapter Seven

Getting Out on Top

From 1976 to 1983, Mike Schmidt played on a contender. During those eight years, the Phillies captured five division titles, two pennants and a world championship. Even in 1981 and 1982, when they didn't win the National League East, the Phillies were in the chase down the stretch. After 1983, though, the team's fortunes changed dramatically. In 1984, the Phils dropped to fourth place and the following year, to fifth. And though in 1986 Schmidt generated excitement with his stellar MVP performance, the Phillies were again out of contention early, finishing a very distant second to the New York Mets—21 and a half games out. Those were difficult seasons for Schmidt. They forced him to reconsider his own passion for the game and to try to find an enjoyment in playing that wasn't tied to the unpleasant reality that the Phillies were no longer a winning club.[1] At times, he became frustrated and publicly criticized management for its lackadaisical approach.

"My overriding goal is to do whatever it takes to get the Phillies organization back on top," he told sports columnist Stan Hochman of the *Philadelphia Daily News* in the spring of 1987. "We're not polished anymore. The minor league system is depleted. The front office has a little to be desired in terms of positions that are held. And the jobs they're doing ... the fields are the worst in the league. The dugouts are filthy. The clubhouse is dirty. The pride factor is not what it used to be. We used to have the best field, now its the worst. We used to have the cleanest dugouts, now they're the dirtiest. We used to have the best minor league system, now it's one of the worst."[2] His candid remarks were not appreciated by the organization, which responded in a patronizing way. When Schmidt arrived in the clubhouse that night, he found green ferns hanging from his locker and candles surrounding his folding chair. Workers were scrubbing the runway from the clubhouse to the dugout in a mock effort to eliminate the smell of "cat piss" Schmidt identified.[3] It wasn't a good situation, especially for Schmidt, who had repeatedly stated his desire to join the brain trust as field manager or general manager after he retired from the game.[4] And he believed retirement was near.

At the end of the 1986 season, Schmidt said that he was "90 percent sure" that the next season would be his last. The physical demands of the game were taking their toll. His chronically aching knees were telling him it was time to leave. Having had four major knee operations, the third baseman was already icing them down before and after playing each day. He certainly didn't want to go through a fifth operation that might jeopardize his ability to walk.[5] Schmidt also wanted to go out on top, with the very same class he had demonstrated throughout his career. "I guess I could play another two or three years," he admitted, "but then I couldn't be counted on for the second game of a doubleheader, or days after travel days. I just don't see myself going out like that."[6]

Another major factor was how his family would feel about "living through another few seasons."[7] For seven months out of the year, Schmidt was away from home. That, of itself, placed a lot of pressure on his wife Donna, who was left to raise their children alone. "The highs are pretty neat," she admitted, "but the lows ... oh my God! You realize that baseball has given you everything you have, and you're very grateful for that. But there's also the negatives, that seem to happen every year—the nagging injuries, the hitting slumps even you don't understand, and the intrusive publicity."[8] Immediately after Christmas, Donna would have to make the adjustment as her husband prepared to leave for spring training. "You know you're not the most important thing anymore," she added. "I think that's the hardest thing, to realize that he can leave you so easily. He has to leave because he is being paid megabucks. It would be wonderful if he could say, 'Honey, you don't feel well, I won't go in today.' But he can't do that. So, whether we like it or not, we're not the most important thing when the season starts, and that's hard to accept sometimes."[9]

Donna was concerned about creating a family atmosphere for their children when for so much of the year, for so many years, Jessica and Jonathan were without a father. "I came to a point where I had to make a decision between the children and Mike," she said. "My children's schedule is more important to me than sitting at a ballgame with 60,000 other people. I love watching Michael play, but the children need me more. Besides, you get tired of living their ups and downs, their wins and losses. You get tired of it because there's nothing you can do about those things."[10]

Nor was Schmidt's demanding schedule or his profession easy on his children, Jonathan, who was six years old, and Jessica, who was eight. When their father struggled through a hitting slump, they heard about it from a peer at school who would say, "Your dad had a bad game last night, isn't he getting a little old?" While the children may have been repeating the sentiments of their fathers, it was still hurtful, especially to youngsters whose love for their own father was unconditional.[11] The effect his playing career was having on his children weighed heavily on Schmidt. Having to be on the road all summer, he never had the luxury of a family vacation during that time. With Jonathan beginning Little League baseball, Schmidt would have to forfeit the opportunity to see him play. In short, the Phillies' third baseman realized he was missing some of the most endearing moments a parent experiences with his children, and he was beginning to have serious reservations about relinquishing any more of those moments in the future.

Financial considerations never played a part in his thinking. The 1987 season represented the last year of his $10 million contract, the final obligation he had to the Phillies. He certainly "didn't need to keep playing for the money."[12] His agent, Arthur Rosenberg, had already made certain that his family's future was insured through prudent investment counseling and a budget that easily met all of his client's financial needs.[13] Phillies President Bill Giles realized that it would take more than another lucrative contract to retain his star third baseman's services. Giles acknowledged Schmidt's desire to go out on top. After all, the Phillies' president didn't relish having to release Pete Rose or Steve Carlton, both of whom, in his mind, hung on too long. But Giles was persistent in his attempt to convince his star third baseman to "play through 1989," telling him that "he could be the player of the decade."[14]

As he went through spring training, Schmidt began to waver on his decision. He adopted a wait-and-see attitude. "Let's face it," he admitted, "playing major league baseball is a very good occupation. It's an easy thing to say that this will be my last season. But the final decision will be a very difficult one. It will be tough to say, 'I'm retiring.' I guess it'll come down to what it has always come down to for me. If I feel good about playing physically, if I feel that my family would be best served by playing, then I'll keep playing. And what the club looks like will have a strong influence on my decision. If we're going to be a contender for the next few years, then that would make it a lot easier to stay. So, basically, it's in God's hands. I'm going to go as far as He wants me to go."[15]

At the same time, Schmidt took action to pave the way for a future in Phillies' pinstripes. He campaigned to have Giles sign free agent Lance Parrish, an All-Star catcher with the Detroit Tigers. Schmidt realized that the Phils needed another 30 home run hitter if the team was going to contend. Giles agreed and signed Parrish. Schmidt also began exploring a new contract with his boss. Having done that, he prepared himself to achieve a major milestone—hitting his five hundredth career home run.

Entering the 1987 season, Schmidt had collected 495 home runs over the course of his 15-year career. That total ranked him fourteenth among the all-time major league home run hitters, behind Hank Aaron (755), Babe Ruth (714), Willie Mays (660), Frank Robinson (586), Harmon Killebrew (573), Reggie Jackson (548), Mickey Mantle (536), Jimmie Foxx (534), Ted Williams and Willie McCovey (both with 521), Eddie Mathews and Ernie Banks (both with 512), and Mel Ott (511). He had already captured the National League home run title eight times, having hit 35 or more homers in each of ten previous seasons. And his career home run ratio of 14.73 ranked Schmidt fourth on the all-time list, behind Babe Ruth (11.76), Ralph Kiner (14.11) and Harmon Killebrew (14.22).[16]

Schmidt attributed his success to the "flexible approach" he took to hitting. "I've always been a student of hitting, watching other players' styles, adopting different techniques if I think they will be more successful," he said. "When I first came into the game in the 1970s, I stood reasonably close to the plate and pulled the ball to left field. I hoped that 30 of those balls would go out of the park and that I would hit 100 RBIs. Sure, I had some success. But I also struck out 150 times a season and hit .250. So I decided to adopt a different style. By standing deeper in the batter's box, I was able to stride into the pitch and hit the ball to all fields. The change allowed me to hit for average, and yet didn't take anything away from my power."[17] Schmidt also believed that the new approach allowed him to become a better team player. By suppressing a desire for personal glory—which is difficult for so many power hitters—he was able to target his hitting performance for the good of the team, while also eliminating some of the pressure he might have felt to hit the long ball.[18] That "team-first" philosophy became apparent during the early part of the regular season.

By April 17, the Phils were 1–8 and languishing in last place in the National League East. Schmidt hit home runs 496, 497 and 498 in losing causes.[19] The Phils would turn it around in a weekend series against Pittsburgh, thanks to Schmidt's hot bat. Home run number 499 came off the Pirates' Bob Patterson in the second inning of the Friday night opener on April 18. It tied the game 1–1 and provided the boost the Phillies needed to go on and win the contest, 6-2, in ten innings.[20]

Shortly before that game, Schmidt phoned his wife and said, "If you want to see my 500th home run, you'd better fly out to Pittsburgh. I can't guarantee that I won't hit it, and I know I'll be disappointed if you weren't here." Despite the fact that Donna had just gotten over a virus, she still said she would try to be there for her husband the following day. "When Michael phoned, I was in the kitchen with my mother," she recalled. "I had been sick to my stomach two days before, Jessica had had it, and Jonathan was throwing up all the day. He was still running a fever, sitting there in my lap. The phone rang and I said to my mother, 'Uh-oh, it's him and he's going to want me to fly to Pittsburgh.' My mother looked at me and said, 'Now dammit, you have no excuse! I'm here and he wants you to be there and you better be there!'"[21] The following morning, Donna said good-bye to her children, boarded a plane and flew to Pittsburgh. She arrived at Three Rivers Stadium just in time for her husband's first at-bat.

The Phillies held a 5–0 lead going into the eighth inning, but the Pirates rallied and took the lead on a three-run homer by Johnny Ray in the bottom of that inning. With one out and the score at 6–5 in the top of the ninth, Juan Samuel broke up a game-ending double play and the Phils began a two-out rally. Von Hayes followed with a walk, bringing Schmidt to the plate. Pirate hurler Don Robinson threw a fastball outside for ball one. His next delivery was low for ball two. The third pitch was also low for ball three.

Schmidt, who hadn't had a good at-bat since hitting his last home run the previous night, stepped out of the batter's box to gather his thoughts. "I'm standing there thinking, 'I've got to get relaxed. Get "home run" out of your mind,'" he recalled. "I knew we didn't need a home run to win the game, just a single. I knew if I got a good pitch to hit on 3 and 0, I was going to try and hit a line drive."[22]

Schmidt took a deep breath, stepped back into the box, tapped home plate and cocked the bat high, readying himself for Robinson's next delivery. The Pittsburgh reliever challenged him with another fastball, but this one tailed in over the center of the plate. Schmidt launched the ball deep into left field. It careened off the concrete wall next to a banner that read, "Pirate Pride," landing harmlessly behind the outfield fence. Phils' broadcaster Harry Kalas, who had witnessed every one of Schmitty's blasts, screamed, "Long drive! There it is! Number 500! Michael Jack Schmidt!"

As the Phillies' third baseman took off for first base, he watched the ball disappear. After it cleared the fence, he high-stepped his way to the bag. Letting go of any inhibitions he might have had, he freely showed his emotions in a display that would become as memorable as his jubilant leap into the arms of his teammates after the final out of the 1980 World Series. As he rounded third base, his teammates jockeyed for position to see who'd be the first to congratulate him. Outfielder Glen Wilson, a good friend of Schmidt's, elbowed his way up the third base line and gave his teammate a double high five.

When the Phillies took the field in the bottom of the ninth to seal their 8–6 victory, Schmidt was called on to play shortstop. In one of the most notable understatements of his career, he later said that returning to his former position was "the greatest thing that happened" that day.[23]

After the game, Harry Kalas underscored the importance of Schmidt's dramatic home run. "This ballclub had lost the game," he admitted. "I mean it might have taken them a month to recover after losing a 5–0 lead. It could have been devastating. I don't think you could find a better storybook ending than Michael Jack's home run."[24] Jim Leyland, manager of the Pirates, echoed Kalas' sentiments. "I just think for special athletes, there are special dramatics," he said of Schmidt's milestone home run. "I'm sure Mike Schmidt is happier today because it was a home run that meant a win for his team, and that says a lot for Mike Schmidt."[25]

Schmidt was humble in his remarks to the press in the postgame interviews. He acknowledged his respect for Don Robinson as "a great pitcher" whom he'd "take on my team anytime."[26] After calling the blast the "greatest thrill of my lifetime," the third baseman expressed his gratefulness to God for the good fortune he experienced in his career. "When I started this game," he recalled, "I said to myself, 'If I stay sound, if I work hard, if God's hand is behind me, then great things can happen.' That's been my attitude my whole life."[27] It was an exemplary statement for a man who had led an exemplary life. Moreover, Schmidt intended to fulfill his obligation as a role model to youngsters, taking advantage of all the media attention he was getting.

At the beginning of the season he announced his support for a United Way Youth Services program that would "give youngsters positive alternatives to the pitfalls of substance abuse." Those corporate sponsors who signed on to the campaign would donate $100 for every home run Schmidt hit that season. Additionally, he launched the campaign with a personal contribution of $10,000.[28] He also agreed to star in a commercial for the National Institute on Drug Abuse of the Department of Health and Human Services. The TV spot, which featured a close-up of Schmidt against a shadowy background, was meant to be a sobering message for impressionable young minds. He delivered his point in a firm, clearly articulated fashion: "I don't need drugs. I believe in me and my ability. I don't want anything interfering with the way I play the game. Cocaine is no way to believe in yourself. It can kill you! If you're into cocaine, get off it! You're living a lie. Get off it while you still have a life!"[29]

Together with his Hall of Fame achievements on the field, Schmidt's concern for young people earned him the respect and admiration of teammates and opponents alike. Cy Young Award winner Rick Sutcliffe of the Cubs, who surrendered home run 497, admitted that Mike was "one of the few players in this game I really respect on and off the field." "I'd love to have had a chance to play on the same team with him," he added. "He does so much for the game. I think his commercial on drug abuse, for example, shows the kind of person he really is. That's not Mike Schmidt the ballplayer talking. That's his heart talking. That's the father and the husband. I just think there should be another league for people like Mike Schmidt."[30] Gary Carter of the Mets agreed, saying that Schmidt was a "class person" and a "thinking man's player."[31]

His teammates were in awe of not only Schmidt's achievements, but of his presence in the clubhouse, as well. For some, the slugger's feats were so legendary and his demeanor so private that it was difficult to approach him. Perhaps pitcher Shane Rawley explained those feelings best when he said that Schmidt was "hard to get to know because he's such a private person and loves to be with his family."[32] At the same time, Rawley admitted that his teammate "likes being 'one of the guys,'" but it was difficult for him to "really let loose because of who he is." "That may sound funny," added the Phillies' hurler, "but he can be very serious at times, maybe too serious. Then again, that seriousness is what makes him stand above the other players." Whatever the case, his teammates all agreed that Schmidt was "one of the finest human beings" in baseball, always willing to give them advice or an encouraging word if they requested it.[33]

Even the fans finally seemed to warm to Schmidt. Nothing he could do was wrong anymore. If he struck out with the bases loaded, the Phillies' faithful seemed to overlook it. There was no more booing, no more talk about "Mr. Cool," the "iceman" of the Phillies' infield. "I think they've always accepted me as a good ballplayer," Schmidt reasoned. "But I also think the fact that I've reached the 500 home run plateau has made them step back and regroup. When you start telling Phillies' fans that 'one of their own' has done something like that, they sit back and say, 'Wait a minute. No kidding? All that has been happening right in front of our eyes? I didn't know that. I was too busy booing him!'"[34]

In late May, Schmidt suffered a pulled rib cage muscle and was forced to go on the fifteen-day disabled list. When he returned to the lineup on June 15 against the Montreal Expos, the power-hitting third baseman picked up where he left off. He hit three homers in that game, pacing the Phillies to an 11–6 victory.[35] It wasn't enough to save his manager's job, though. The team had been playing listlessly. The following day, Felske was fired and replaced with coach Lee Elia, a career man with the Phils. Under his leadership, the team didn't fare much better, going 51–50 for the remainder of the season. Schmidt enjoyed another splendid year, hitting .293 with 35 HR and 113 RBIs, and was selected to the All-Star team for the eleventh time in his career. But his best seasons were now behind him.[36] So it also seemed for the Phillies.

Von Hayes (.277 avg., 21 HR, 84 RBI), Glenn Wilson (.264 avg., 14 HR, 54 RBI) and Lance Parrish (.245 avg., 17 HR, 67 RBI) did not produce the numbers or the power-hitting they were expected to deliver. Nor was the pitching very solid. Aside from reliever Steve Bedrosian (5–3, 2.83 ERA, 40 saves), who won the Cy Young Award, the most consistent hurler was Rawley (17–11, 123 K, 4.38 ERA). Bruce Ruffin (11–14, 93 K, 4.35 ERA), who took Steve Carlton's place in the rotation the previous season, put up some respectable numbers, but would never again win more than six games in a season with the Phils and was traded four years later. The Phillies finished in fourth place, 15 games out.[37] Nevertheless, Schmidt felt the Phils could rebound from the disappointing season and be a contender in the near future. In fact, he was so confident of that belief that he signed a new, two-year contract worth $4.5 million with the team.[38]

Unfortunately, Bill Giles made the announcement of the new deal with some ambivalent feelings. On one hand, he called Schmidt "the greatest third baseman that's ever played this game" and maybe even "the *best player* that's ever played this game." On the other, Giles was critical of his star player's leadership ability, insisting that while Schmidt was "intelligent enough to be a leader, he's so moody."[39] It was a statement that echoed former manager John Felske's remark that the team would "never have a true leader until Schmidt retired" because "the young players were intimidated by him" and were "trying too hard to emulate him."[40] Instead of taking exception to the statement, Schmidt agreed with it. "Moody's probably not that far off in terms of describing me," he admitted. "However, I think we all have that label at times. There's not a player around who has the ideal mood. Although I'm totally satisfied with myself in terms of my behind-the-scenes leadership, my approach to the game, my leading by example, I guess I have to pat a few more butts and do a little more screaming in the clubhouse. I know that most of the young players on the team are a little scared of me. I've done my best to try to ease the pressure of that situation. I've been out to dinner with every kid on the team. Still, it's human nature. I mean, ten years ago, if I were playing with Hank Aaron, I'd be thinking, 'I've got to watch what I do, what I say.' So, maybe the best thing for me to do is let leadership happen more naturally."[41]

While the responsibility for leadership was placed squarely on Schmidt's shoulders, it was unfair to ask him to change. Leadership comes in a variety of forms. Schmidt's style was to lead by example in the way he prepared for the game and the way he played it. He wasn't going to be a Pete Rose, or a Larry Bowa, or a Lenny Dykstra, no matter how hard others wanted him to be. It just wasn't his personality. The fact that he was a future Hall of Famer was intimidating to his teammates, and there was nothing he could do about that. Nor should he. After all, he earned that reputation and deserved it.

What made the situation worse, however, is that the Phillies were playing poorly from the very start of the season. Schmidt's performance was partly to blame. He was hitting only .236 by the beginning of June with home run (five) and RBI (32) totals that were uncharacteristically low. His play at third base was just as dismal, having committed ten errors. Elia considered moving Schmidt back to first base and turning over the hot corner to Von Hayes.[42] The fans, the press and the front office were beginning to wonder if his reflexes were beginning to go. Even Schmidt wondered whether he should have retired after the previous season. "There should be questions about me," he admitted. "Am I a DH now? Am I starting to decline? I wouldn't deny that. Hey, I'm human. It's human nature for me to be concerned. I'm concerned enough to wonder whether this is the big one."[43]

Predictably, the media began their Schmidt-bashing, the most damaging article appearing in the premier issue of *Philly Sport* in late June. In a muckraking article titled "Even Superstars Get the Blues," sportswriter Bruce Buschel sarcastically criticized Schmidt for everything from his low-key personality to what he perceived to be a self-aggrandizing treatment of young, impressionable fans. The essay was malicious, crafted with the intention to embarrass Schmidt. Playing the role of amateur psychologist, Buschel wrote: "If art is something that continuously gives you back more than you bring to

it, then Mike Schmidt is no masterpiece. He demands too much. He is ener-
vating. If baseball is where you go for simplicity, for good and bad, Schmidt
dishes out ambiguity. He can win and lose at the same time. He can have the
confidence to be Mike Schmidt and still be uncertain of his gifts. Somehow,
this immortal player never fails to remind us of our own mortality. Athletes
are not supposed to be wracked with the same doubts and fears as the rest of
us; most need to block them out to perform. Schmidt seems to need them.
He emanates neuroses. He blames the fans; he thanks the fans. They helped
him; they hurt him. Sometimes, he appears so conflicted that he's paralyzed
by crossed emotions. Or he looks bored. Bored!"[44]

Buschel's piece was distinguished by selective quotation and a myopic
view that professional athletes have no right to be human beings, to express
their own disappointment when they and even their families are treated so
mean-spiritedly by the fans or the media. At best, the article was irresponsi-
bly written; at worst, hostile and defaming. It represented the negative side
of the schizophrenic treatment the press had given Schmidt over the course
of his 17-year career. There were, however, those sportswriters who were more
objective.

Frank Dolson and Bill Lyon of the *Philadelphia Inquirer* distinguished
themselves for such fair-minded treatment. When Schmidt deserved to be
criticized for an inappropriate remark, they did so. At the same time, they
were more sympathetic during his slumps than their colleagues, realizing that
he pressed himself harder than any of his contemporaries. Season after season, Dolson and Lyon were the most consistent of all Philadelphia's sportswriters in their coverage of Schmidt.[45]

In the midst of all the criticism and his poor play came the announcement that Bill Giles hired Lee Thomas, director of player development for
the St. Louis Cardinals, as the Phils' new general manager. Giles himself had
previously held the position and there was some speculation that he might
have been holding it for Schmidt to fill when the slugger retired. That possibility was dashed with the hiring of Thomas. Just as obvious was that mas-
sive changes were needed in the organization as the Phillies headed for another
poor finish, this time in sixth place, 35 and a half games out.

Thomas made immediate changes. Before the season ended, he fired Lee
Elia and named former Cardinal coach Nick Leyva manager. He traded unpro-
ductive veterans like Lance Parrish for younger prospects and began revamp-
ing the minor league and scouting systems.[46] One of the biggest questions
that loomed on the horizon was whether to retain Schmidt or buy out the final
year of his contract for $300,000.

Schmidt, who missed the last six weeks of the season with a rotator cuff
injury, insisted he would be "ready to play next year" and "just might have
his best year ever."[47] After finishing the 1988 campaign with a .249 average
and only 12 home runs and 62 RBIs, Giles was less optimistic. Schmidt was

39 years old and would have to undergo an arthroscopic operation to mend his torn rotator cuff, an injury that could hamper his hitting ability. Nevertheless, Giles continued to hold talks with Schmidt's agent, Arthur Rosenberg, through the fall in the hope that the third baseman would finish his career in Philadelphia.[48] For Schmidt, who spent part of that time lying in a hospital bed recuperating from surgery, the talks were inextricably linked to the issue of loyalty. "I've undergone an operation because of what I've done for the Phillies," he reasoned. "I think in return for that, they should at least be tolerant toward my situation. There ought to be a sense of loyalty."[49]

The Phillies decided not to pick up the option on his contract—which would have paid him $2.25 million—and instead offered him a pact with a guaranteed salary of $300,000 and potential earnings of $1.7 million if he met certain incentives. Schmidt rejected the offer and filed for free agency.[50] It wasn't a negotiating tactic as much as a matter of pride.

Several teams expressed interest in him, including the New York Yankees, the Cincinnati Reds and the Los Angeles Dodgers. New York had an appeal to Schmidt because of its proximity to his suburban Philadelphia home.[51] Cincinnati also held a special attraction because of his friendship with Reds manager Pete Rose, who was actively campaigning to have him as the team's regular first baseman.[52] However, Rosenberg, understanding Schmidt's strong desire to remain a Phillie, continued negotiations with Giles and Thomas. Finally, on December 7, Schmidt and the Phillies came to an agreement on a one-year contract that would guarantee him $500,000, with incentives that could add up to a potential package of $2.05 million.[53]

When all was said and done, Schmidt was happy that he would be returning to the Phillies. "I really ran the gamut of emotions through this whole thing," he admitted at the press conference announcing his new deal. "I had a very good understanding of the Phillies' position with me. I mean, I kind of stand out like a sore thumb on this ballclub—in terms of what I'm making, in terms of my age, in terms of the way the organization is planning to go the next two or three years, in terms of what they could get for me as free agent compensation if I did sign with somebody else. I could have wound up in another city. I could have ended up not playing anywhere. There were a lot of things on the down side of these negotiations that were different than the other ones. But in the end, I think the issue of loyalty was the real reason I ended up back where I wanted to be the whole time, anyway."[54]

Schmidt also addressed the issue of leadership and his realization that he would have to be more proactive with his teammates and less reactive with the public in the future. "I don't know if I can ever change people's images of me," he said, conceding that he knew there were those people in the organization who wanted him to leave. "I can't change my career—what I've accomplished, what I've done. I'm a family man. I'm a clean living man. The way I play, I try to be an example to kids. And I probably want more than anybody in the Phillies organization to win—more than Bill Giles, more than the owners, more than anybody."

"But maybe I'm at fault for that. Over the years, in the many times I've been interviewed, I've told the truth—as I see it. And that probably has hurt a few people, including myself, from time to time. I've got to contain those opinions now. I've got to be a little more concerned about those kinds of things. I see that now. I've learned a lesson."[55]

With Schmidt's return, Nick Leyva found himself in an unenviable position. He was a first-year manager trying to put a competitive team on the field. The logical position for the 39-year-old slugger would be first base, but the Phils had already made a commitment to Ricky Jordan, a prospect whose .308 average, 11 HR and 43 RBI in just 69 games the previous year made him a good bet to be the team's cleanup hitter of the future. Jordan's one weakness was his throwing arm and that meant he could play nowhere but first base.[56] Leyva also had three younger players, Chris James, Von Hayes, and Steve Jeltz, who could step in to play third base. Predictably, Thomas and Leyva scrutinized Schmidt's performance throughout spring training, and it wasn't impressive. He struggled both in the field and at the plate. Despite the fact that he had gone 1-for-18 and hadn't hit a single home run through the first half of the Grapefruit League schedule, management gave him the nod at third base. It was the only fair thing to do.

"If this were a situation of two kids going for the same job, Chris James would have beat him out," admitted Thomas. "But that isn't the situation. A veteran player cannot be judged on spring training. From the beginning, I've operated on the assumption that if Mike couldn't do the job, he'd know that and come to us. Since he hasn't come to us, he obviously thinks he still can do it. If we go into the season and he shows us that he can't do the job, then we'll have some decisions to make."[57] Leyva echoed Thomas' sentiments. "Of course I had my doubts about Mike coming into the spring," he admitted. "But he's busted his tail and is determined to get himself back together again. He's going to hit fourth in our lineup and, offensively, if he can still do the job like I think he can, he's going to drive in a lot of runs and help our club."[58] Schmidt, who had grown tired of being scrutinized by the media and the brain trust, was comfortable with that strategy, promising that he'd "retire" if he couldn't achieve "the high standards" he'd always set for himself. Those standards meant being on pace for a 35 HR and 110 RBI season.[59] Clearly the Phillies weren't expecting that. They would be happy if he could give the team 20 to 25 homers and drive in 90 runs.

Schmidt kept his word. After a solid April, in which he hit five home runs and collected 22 RBIs, he went into a month-long tailspin. His fielding had deteriorated. There was very little consistency in his performance at the plate. The team was languishing in last place. Players came and went with such regularity that it was difficult to know who was on the roster at any given time. At the end of May, Schmidt was hitting just .203 with only one homer for the month. That homer, the last of his brilliant career, came at Veterans Stadium on May 2 off the Houston Astros. Finally, on Sunday, May 28, the third baseman reached his decision to retire after the Phils' 8–5 loss to San Francisco, where his own error preceded a game-winning grand slam by Giants first baseman Will Clark. It was the team's fifth straight loss—and their ninth in eleven games—on what proved to be a dismal trip to the West Coast.[60]

During a hastily arranged news conference the following day before the Phillies' game against the San Diego Padres, Schmidt made the announcement. Stating that he had always set high standards for himself as a player and that he believed he could "no longer perform up to those standards," he admitted, "I feel like I could ask the Phillies to make me a part-time player in order to hang around for a couple years and add to my statistical totals. However, my respect for the game, my teammates and the fans won't allow me to do that."

Schmidt paused to compose himself, then continued: "The Phillies are a first-class organization and have always supported me with loyalty and security that few players, if any, will ever know. For that, I will be forever thankful to the Philadelphia Phillies."

Fighting back tears, he said, "You probably won't believe this, by the way I look right now, but this is a joyous time for me. I've had a great career. My family and friends and I are very content and excited about my decision. It's the beginning of a new life focus."

Schmidt tried to collect himself again. "Some eighteen years ago, I left Dayton, Ohio, with two very bad knees and a dream to become a major league baseball player," he concluded, as he began to cry. "I thank God that the dream came true."[61]

Unable to compose himself any longer, Schmidt broke down, sobbing uncontrollably. Phillies President Bill Giles took over the microphone. "Thank you from the bottom of my heart, and for all the Phillies fans who have seen you play for over 16 years," he continued. "In my opinion, you're the greatest third baseman of all time. It's been a real honor and pleasure to have seen you play."

Giles was somber, but dignified in his remarks.

"I think all of us who have followed your career will be grateful not only for what you did on the field, but for the way you lived your life off the field," he added. "And I think that's just as important."[62]

It was an emotional announcement for Schmidt, a man who had always kept his emotions in check from the general public. Perhaps that is why it was so memorable.

Less than 24 hours later, Schmidt found himself standing at home plate at Veterans Stadium, giving another press conference. Trying to explain his decision to retire, he admitted that it was "the toughest thing I had to do in

Schmidt wipes away tears at a May 29, 1989, press conference in San Diego, where he announced his retirement from baseball. Stating his belief that he could "no longer perform up to the high standards he had set for himself as a player," the Phillie third baseman decided to retire because of his "respect for the game." (*Courtesy of AP/Wide World Photos.*)

my life" and that he had "prayed about it, asking the Lord to give [him] a sign" that he should keep playing. But after four or five games he was "getting nothing but signs that [he] should retire." Dismissing the celebrity status, million dollar salaries, and jet-set lifestyle as "such a small part of baseball," he described with moving eloquence the true meaning of being a major leaguer. "It's the feeling you have for those three hours when you're standing out there, that's what it's all about. And I knew that feeling had left." When asked if he would come out of retirement if a contending team requested his services, Schmidt responded with an emphatic "no."[63]

Then the future Hall of Famer tried to explain what had been, for so many years, the inexplicable for the fans and the media. Giving some personal insight into the struggle he waged with his own ego, Schmidt candidly admitted, "I longed to be a great major league baseball player and have people want my autograph. I wanted all the things that young players want. But I wasn't sure I had the confidence. I wasn't sure I was man enough to do that. I wasn't sure I could do the things I needed to do to stay in the big leagues, to be one of the Philadelphia Phillies forever. I really wasn't sure."

His remarks revealed the humanness that he so desperately tried to shield from the public. But now that it was over, he wanted people to know that the game had not come naturally for him; that he wasn't cool, composed or withdrawn; that he had to *struggle* to stay on top.

"I'm no different than any person who undertakes something in their life that scares them. Of course, the macho feeling, the ego within me wouldn't allow that to surface. I walked around like a cool guy, like a guy who was sure of himself, like nothing bothered me. That was not the case. I was very unsure of myself and probably a little scared. Somehow, the good Lord changed that and made some things happen for me by allowing the Dave Cashes, Dick Allens and Pete Roses to enter into my career. All along the line there were those kinds of people to pat me on the back and say, 'You're going to be a great one.' And as soon as somebody told me that, that's when I took off."[64]

Later that week, before the Phillies took the field against the Atlanta

Schmidt and his wife, Donna, leave Philadelphia's Veterans Stadium after his farewell news conference, May 31, 1989. (*Courtesy of Urban Archives, Temple University, Philadelphia, Pennsylvania.*)

Braves, Mike Schmidt returned to Veterans Stadium to bid farewell to the hometown fans. Emerging from the tunnel behind home plate, he looked resplendent in a cream colored suit, accentuated by a leathery suntan. Although his reddish brown hair was now flecked with gray, he still had an impressive physical appearance. At 6' 2" and 200 pounds, he was a ruggedly handsome man who still looked to have a few career years left in him.

As he made his way to the microphone, the highlights of his playing career flashed on the big screen in center field. The crowd was on its feet, applauding. Flashbulbs were blinking. Surveying the scene in a long, slow circle, Schmidt held up his right hand, acknowledging the cheers. The ovation lasted over a minute. It would have been much longer had he not quieted the crowd. But he was edgy, being uncomfortable with all the praise. As he began to speak, his chiseled features began to show their vulnerability.

"As you know, and I just proved it, none of us have any control over the future in our lives," he began. "All we can do is dream, and hope that God allows us to fulfill our dreams. God allowed me to fulfill my dream.

"I thank you people for being a very, very large part of that dream. The noise you made over the years, the great sounds of approval and those ugly sounds of disapproval, are all part of a career, are all a single part of the whole.

"And I thank God you were here to be a part of my career, to push me to the limit. Thank you so much.

"God bless you all."[65]

A month later Schmidt made baseball history by being the first retired player elected to the All-Star Game. It was a unique tribute, one he said was a "great honor that I'll always remember." Although Schmidt chose not to play in the game, he was introduced along with the other National Leaguers who went to Anaheim, California, that summer.[66] Other accolades followed.

In January 1990, *The Sporting News* named Schmidt the "Player of the Decade." The tribute recognized the fact that the former Phillies' third baseman had achieved more during the decade of the 1980s than any other baseball player. He hit more home runs (313) than anyone else, earned three Most Valuable Player Awards, and played in the World Series twice. He also earned six Gold Gloves, six Silver Slugger Awards, and was named to eight All-Star teams. Saying that it was "extremely flattering" to be recognized as the best player of the 1980s, Schmidt was modest about his accomplishments, tending to emphasize the important role his teammates played in his career.[67] Later that same year, 56,789 fans, family members and former teammates turned out to pay tribute to Mike as the Phillies retired his uniform number 20.[68] It should have been an occasion that laid to rest all of the criticism, the hurtful behavior and unfair remarks that had been directed at Schmidt over the course of his storied career. Unfortunately it wasn't.

Former Phillie Mike Schmidt waves to the crowd at the opening ceremonies of the All-Star Game on July 11, 1989. Though Schmidt retired earlier in the season, he was the leading vote-getter among third basemen and the first player ever voted to an All-Star squad after his retirement. (*Courtesy of UPI/Corbis-Bettmann.***)**

Retirement was difficult at first. Schmidt had often expressed an interest in managing the Phillies or taking a position in the front office. But Phillies President Bill Giles never gave him that opportunity. When asked about the issue, Giles pointed to the track record of retired superstars who tried, unsuccessfully, to manage. Citing Ted Williams and Pete Rose as prime examples, Giles contended that "very few great players have been good management people; that's just a fact. I don't know why that is, except perhaps the game comes so easily to them. They get used to the success and adulation. Being a general manager is more work than they realize. Most great players don't have the patience for it."[69] There was more to it than that, though.

Giles believed that Schmidt intimidated young players and didn't have the kind of patience or personable disposition necessary to handle a young team. "Mike is not a people person," Giles said. "He can appear brusque without realizing it, and that's part of his problem. Communication is a big part of the business, and Mike isn't always a good communicator."[70] Nor did Giles feel that the Phillies "owed" Schmidt anything more than the handsome financial rewards the organization paid him during his playing career.

The rebuff hurt Schmidt deeply. Giles' contention that Schmidt was not a "people person" sounded shallow given all the community service work he had done and the following he did have among his more loyal fans. Those fans understood that Schmidt was a naturally introverted person who tended to speak from the heart. It's a quality that endeared him to them. Schmidt could have chosen to be a parrot for the organization, fabricating a public personality simply to get ahead. But that would have been superficial. He might have chosen to remain silent when he disagreed with management. But that would seem to lack integrity for a man who had made an earnest effort to "do the right thing" in his personal and professional lives. Besides, silence was not an option for a marquee player. The fans and the sportswriters expected him to take a position. Under these circumstances, Giles' remarks to the press are difficult to understand. Not only did they demand a response from Schmidt, but seemed to breach the trust he once placed in the Phillies' president.

In an especially candid interview, Schmidt tried to explain his relationship with the Phillies organization to Ray Didinger of the *Philadelphia Daily News*. Admitting that he was not the best communicator, Schmidt did insist that he spoke "from the heart" and that "talking to reporters is probably the main reason I'm not the [Phillies'] general manager. I'm just not good at editing what I say. I've said a lot of things over the years that ruffled people's feathers, including Bill Giles. But I said what I said because I care about the organization."

"Let me tell you something," he said emphatically. "There's only one guy in this town whose organization that is, and it's mine. Somebody else may own it, but it's mine. I can't think of anyone who cares about the Phillies more than I do. I've worn that uniform longer than anybody. If you don't think I feel a loyalty to the Phillies, then you don't know me. I care. I care a lot."[71] Once again, Schmidt spoke from the heart and, once again, the Philadelphia press ran another of its infamous stories, highlighting the negative and downplaying his contributions to Philadelphia, both on and off the field.[72]

Baseball had been much more than a professional career for him; it had been a large part of his personal identity. That is not unusual for any recently retired player, especially a superstar. According to Dr. Joel Fish of the Center for Sports Psychology in Philadelphia and the sports psychologist for the Phillies organization, retiring players have "an understandable sense of loss when their careers are over." They experience all the emotions that "come along with a sense of loss, which typically include denial, anger and sadness." Some are able to come to terms with those feelings. Others continue to "have one foot in the past and one in the present because either there's some unfinished business in their career or they just haven't been able to find the same rush, the same charge in their postathletic life."[73]

Schmidt was struggling with all those mixed emotions. Had he been a Joe DiMaggio, who played with the same graceful style, people would have understood him. In fact, if a player of Schmidt's caliber played in any other city, he might have been given a statue in front of the stadium and any job he wanted in the organization. But in Philadelphia, it's a different story. In the City of Brotherly Love, owners interpret "loyalty" in dollars and cents. Fans tend to ask, "What have you done for me lately?" Sportswriters tend to "bait" and "bash" franchise players, and Schmidt had always been an especially attractive target during his playing days, so why not continue their little game in his retirement?

Schmidt tried to remain in the game in other ways. He accepted the Phillies' offer to join their cable broadcast team as a commentator.[74] He offered to tutor his young successor, Charlie Hayes, at third base and even offered to manage in the minor leagues for however little money the Phillies wanted to pay him.[75] Again, the offers were declined.

Despite the rebuffs, Schmidt continued his community service involvement in Philadelphia by sponsoring the "Mike Schmidt–Philadelphia Newspapers Inc. Charity Golf Tournament." When the celebrity-studded event failed to raise the $100,000 it promised to the Pennsylvania Special Olympics, Schmidt even offered to pay the charity out of his own pocket. Once again, the press had a field day, criticizing Schmidt for failing to "live up to a promise."[76] Undeterred by the criticism, Schmidt continued to host the tournament and made certain that the Special Olympics received the money it was promised. Unfortunately, that didn't warrant the same kind of press coverage in the eyes of the sportswriters.

In 1993, Schmidt moved his family to Jupiter, Florida, and began a new, less scrutinized life. He took the competitive skills he learned from professional baseball and parlayed them into a business career, first with Golden Bear Enterprises, Jack Nicklaus's athletic management company, and later with his own retail boat dealership, Waterway Marine. He also found great personal enjoyment in golf.

"There's just no place for me in the Phillies organization for me right now," he said before leaving. "I understand that. I'll always feel I could have helped people in baseball after I finished playing. But if it didn't happen immediately after my retirement, it wasn't going to happen."[77]

It was a very sad statement, not so much for Schmidt, but about the Phillies organization. Instead of trying to understand him and settling their differences privately—without the press—the Phillies had distanced themselves from the greatest player in their history.

Chapter Eight

Cooperstown: July 30, 1995

Sunday, July 30, 1995, dawned clear and crisp on the shore of Otsego Lake. A cool breeze chilled the morning air of Cooperstown, the sleepy little village in upstate New York where baseball was supposedly born.[1] Already the first carloads of Philadelphians were descending on the bucolic town, an enduring shrine to the immortals, many of whom once donned the pinstripes of the New York Yankees. But on this day, Cooperstown belonged to the Phillies' faithful. Two of their own would be inducted into the National Baseball Hall of Fame that afternoon.

It would be an affair to remember for two generations—those who lived and died with Rich Ashburn, the sparkplug of the 1950 National League Champion Whiz Kids who now broadcast the team's games, and a younger breed who had schizophrenically booed and cheered, loved and hated Michael Jack Schmidt, the greatest third baseman ever to play the game.

To qualify for the Hall of Fame, a player must be retired from the game for five years, have played ten years in the majors and made a significant contribution to the game. If he then receives votes on 75 percent of the ballots cast by the Baseball Writers of America, he joins the select few who enjoy the highest honor that can be bestowed on a baseball player—induction into the Hall of Fame. Those who receive the honor are awarded more than a bronze plaque; they are granted baseball immortality.

Schmidt's election was a foregone conclusion, the only question being whether it would be unanimous. Unfortunately, it wasn't. He was named on 444 of 460 ballots cast by the Baseball Writers, which gave him the fourth highest percentage of the vote in history.[2] Predictably, there were those Philadelphia sportswriters who, out of personal animosity, took issue with Schmidt's candidacy.[3] The purposeful snub did not deter him, though. He was gracious and humble about the honor, saying that it "took his breath away" to "be considered in the same light" as the other immortals.[4]

**Donald Marr (left) and Ed Stack of the National Baseball Hall of Fame present
Mike Schmidt with his plaque during induction ceremonies at Cooperstown, New
York, on July 30, 1995. (*Courtesy of National Baseball Hall of Fame Library*.)**

That sunny Sunday in July would be a time to mend fences, forget about
the hurtful things of the past, and focus on the memorable moments. By 2:00
P.M. that afternoon, a sea of red Phillies caps had flocked to the spacious
grounds surrounding the Clark Sports Center, where the induction ceremony
would be held. Somewhere between 25,000 and 28,000 fans had made the
four and a half hour trek from Philadelphia to honor their heroes, making it
the largest turnout ever.[5]

When it was his turn to make his acceptance speech, Schmidt delivered
a thoughtful, statesmanlike address. "Thank you, thank you," he began, clearly
in awe of the gathering. "What a great day. I only wish that all of you out
there could stand right here and see what I'm looking at. It's truly amazing."[6]

After congratulating Ashburn and the other inductees—Vic Willis, Leon
Day and William Hulbert—Schmidt admitted how moved he was by the occasion. "I really do stand before you a man that's totally humbled by the mag-
nitude of this entire experience. It's unbelievable. To be honored at this historic
annual baseball ritual is truly the finishing touch on what was an extremely
rewarding career."

As he had done so often before in ceremonies that honored his playing
achievements, Schmidt acknowledged those people who made it all possible,
beginning with his grandmother who "used to pitch me a tennis ball in the
backyard" when he was a youngster. He also thanked his parents, wife and

children for their unconditional love and support over the years of his career. Others he thanked included his college coach, Bob Wren; Tony Lucadello, who scouted him for the Phillies; and Paul Owens, Andy Seminick, Granny Hamner, Garry Maddox, Andre Thornton, Ruly Carpenter, Bill Giles, Danny Ozark, Dallas Green and Arthur Rosenberg. He gave a special thanks to Pete Rose, who, in 1989, had been banned from baseball for life by then-commissioner Bart Giamatti for illegal gambling.[7]

Rose declined to attend the ceremony, not wanting to divert any attention from his good friend.[8] Schmidt expressed his hope "that some day very soon" his former teammate "will be standing right here." When the huge crowd roared its approval, the Phillies' Hall of Fame third baseman half-jokingly replied, "I know y'all agree with me on that one. It's great that we see eye to eye on something, isn't it, Philadelphia?"

Then he addressed his "misunderstood" relationship with the fans. "Can we put that to rest here today?" he asked. "I and my family sure hope that we can."

"Sure, there were tough nights and tough games at Vet Stadium," he continued. "You've got to realize that that's the nature of the sport we play. But I remember most your cheers of anticipation as I would come to the plate for a big at-bat. The curtain calls after big home runs. And that number 20 being hung on the outfield wall at Vet Stadium forever. And that's the bottom line. Just like today, you're here. Back then, you were there, and I know you cared. For that I thank you."

It was a valiant effort to forgive and forget.

Schmidt then delivered a powerful message about the current state of the game he loved, emphasizing the honor and responsibility of preserving the national pastime for generations to come.

"I considered playing professional baseball a privilege, a privilege that is granted to only a few men," he said. "It is my sense that many of today's players are taking that privilege for granted. A game that at one time was steeped with passion, humility and respect for the opposition has now given way to the 'look-at-me, in-your-face' attitude."

"Our game has reached a crossroads," he continued. "I don't believe it can survive unless the team owners and players become one. Take a look at the empty seats in the stadiums, or drive by an empty playground where kids used to be playing ball. That concerns me. And, baseball, that should scare you."

He went on to challenge the players and owners to find a new commissioner, one who might build an amicable relationship between the two sides and help to restore the integrity of the game.

Finally, Schmidt gave some parting advice to the children in the crowd, advice he had lived by throughout his life.

"Never stop chasing your dreams," he urged. "Your dreams are your best

While Schmidt may have been criticized for an inability to lead on the field, he was one of baseball's most admired role models. An active fund-raiser for the United Way, the Philadelphia Child Guidance Clinic and the Christian Children's Fund, he took his responsibility to youngsters very seriously, setting a wonderful example for other athletes. (*Courtesy of the National Baseball Hall of Fame Library.*)

motivators. My career is an example of how you can beat the odds, an example of how someone's dreams can come true. But remember this: In the final analysis, you can believe in your dreams, you can be taught, supported, motivated and loved by others, but, ultimately, your success depends on you. You must take responsibility for your body, your mind and for your character."

To be sure, Mike Schmidt was a natural. He was born with certain abilities that allowed him to excel at the hot corner and at the plate. He had a strong arm with a fairly quick, but very accurate, release. He had excellent reflexes that enabled him to react to hard-hit ground balls to his left and right. He had a fearlessness that allowed him to take the hard-hit liners and one-hops off his body. And he played intelligently. When he knew he had no play at first, for example, Schmidt was known to fake a throw, whirl, and catch the lead runner between second and third. Watching him play third base was captivating not because of what he did as much as how he did it. Schmidt played with such natural grace and intelligence that there was a sense of magic to his performance. It carried over to his hitting as well.

Schmidt was a .270 hitter for most of his major league career. But he will always be remembered for his 548 round trippers. Home run hitting is a science that depends upon much more than brute strength. It takes exceptional hand-eye coordination, quick wrists and timing—abilities that must be bestowed on an individual at birth. You either have them or you don't. Schmidt was blessed with those abilities, which is why he evoked such awe and such excitement. With one swing of his bat, he could decide a game or, as he did in 1980, a season. No wonder Ted Williams recently identified Schmidt as one of the top twenty hitters of all-time. "As a hitter Mike Schmidt was the power and thrust of the whole National League for most of his career," writes baseball's last .400 hitter. "He had the league right where he wanted it, and the pitchers didn't have a clue how to handle him. He was an intelligent hitter who tried to put himself in the pitcher's shoes and think like the pitcher. Stan Musial agrees that Schmidt was the dominant power in his league for a long time. That's good enough for me."[9]

But for all his natural abilities, Schmidt still had an impressive work ethic. He disciplined himself to hit the breaking ball and to cut down on his strikeouts. Later in his career, he reworked his batting style so he could hit for average as well as power. He also redefined himself as a third baseman after a brief hiatus at first. While Schmidt *the power hitter* may have garnered MVP awards in 1980 and 1981, it was Schmidt *the complete ballplayer* who captured a third MVP in 1986. What's more, he did it at the age of 36, when most other players are considering retirement.

As a player, then, the key to Mike Schmidt's success rested with his meticulous approach to hitting and his ability to adapt to change, to "reinvent" himself. Without that kind of work ethic and flexibility, he might have been one slugger in a long procession of power hitters whose stars rose and fell within the span of a few years.

Ultimately, Schmidt's greatest achievement was his consistency, his ability to be one of the very best players in major league baseball for 17 years. By the time he retired, he might have taken a step off the pedestal, but he was still pretty close to the top of his game.

Success was a mixed blessing for him, though. The intrusiveness and unreasonable expectations of both the Philadelphia fans and the media was the price he paid for superstardom. He was loved and hated, glorified and condemned, accused and pardoned, perhaps more than any other professional athlete in Philadelphia's sports history. Despite the schizophrenic treatment, he tried to live up to his obligations as a superstar, especially as a role model to youngsters. Perhaps he did it from a distance. Perhaps he wasn't always as approachable as the fans or the media had hoped. Perhaps his remarks were a bit too candid or were delivered with a poor sense of timing. But he did care about the game, the way he played it and the way he carried himself.

Epilogue

A decade has passed since Mike Schmidt retired from major league baseball. Since that time the Philadelphia Phillies made it to the postseason just once, in 1993. Led by Darren Daulton, Lenny Dykstra and John Kruk, that swaggering, trash-talking bunch went from worst to first in the span of two years and then declined just as rapidly. Anyone who played for, followed or covered the 1993 Phillies would admit that that team enjoyed the rare combination of chemistry, talent and luck that results in extraordinary success. Unfortunately the 1993 Phillies fell just short of being a team of destiny. In Game Six of the World Series, Toronto's Joe Carter dashed their hopes for a second world championship when he rocketed a Mitch Williams fastball into the left field bleachers to give the Blue Jays the title. Aside from that season, the Phillies have enjoyed little success on the playing field since Schmidt's departure.

While the sportswriters are quick to identify bad trades, a depleted farm system and poor scouting as the main reasons for the Phillies' dismal performance, the blame should go to the front office, which operated more from a business standpoint than a baseball one. Of course, it would be naive to think that any franchise can succeed these days without sound business principles. Just as naive, however, is the belief that any organization is going to be consistently successful without knowledgeable baseball men in management. The Atlanta Braves have been in postseason play every year since 1991 because they have both.

To be sure, the Phillies' current management has made some admirable strides in this direction. Dallas Green and Paul Owens, who cultivated the players on the 1980 world championship team, are valuable members of the front office. Both men offer years of experience in management, scouting and evaluation. Ruben Amaro, Jr., a young, well-educated former player, was recently retained to learn the "baseball business" as a special assistant to the general manager. Amaro's role is an extremely important one if the Phillies hope to improve their scouting of Latin American ballplayers; something they

123

have neglected for years. Most admirable is the front office's decision to take the "long-term" approach: identify good, young prospects; strengthen a depleted farm system, especially the pitching; and build a consistent winner for the future. It is the same model Owens and Green followed in building the 1980 championship squad. But the Phillies' still have a serious problem, and it concerns loyalty.

In these days of madcap free agency, dynasties are difficult to establish. But if an organization can identify young players who are committed to the team or city, then the possibility exists to create something special. Currently, very few gifted athletes want to play in Philadelphia. Reggie White left Eagles football for Green Bay. Charles Barkley left Sixers basketball for Phoenix. And baseball's top-ranked draft pick, J. D. Drew, opted to sit out a year and reenter the draft rather than play for the Phillies. If Philadelphia hopes to attract standout prospects or even the big-name free agents, the fans will have to learn to treat those players who deliver for the organization with more respect than they have in the past, and the pro sports teams will have to do a better job of protecting their players from an especially intrusive media. Ultimately, these were the problems that tarnished Mike Schmidt's otherwise brilliant career with the Phillies. They also resulted in his relocating to Florida when his intelligence, experience and commitment could have been valuable assets to Philadelphia and to the Phillies long after his playing days had ended.

Although Schmidt claims he is "very content with [his] current relationship with Philadelphia and the Phillies," it is difficult to believe that he doesn't feel rejected by his former team and city.[1] Given all that he has done for Philadelphia baseball—both on and off the field—he deserves serious consideration for a position within the organization. After all, Schmidt could have taken his Hall of Fame credentials to New York, Cincinnati or Los Angeles on two separate occasions during his 17-year career. But he chose to remain in Philadelphia. He could have snubbed the several community-based organizations that appealed to him for his time, money and endorsement. But he chose to promote them by becoming an active fund-raiser. He could have led the kind of self-indulgent lifestyle of so many other major leaguers in the 1970s and 1980s. But he chose to be a role model for youngsters. All of these contributions were made from a genuine desire to give something back to the city and to the organization that gave him the opportunity to become a major league baseball player.

To be sure, the Phillies paid Mike Schmidt handsomely for his efforts on the field. Nor is Schmidt without blame in the current state of affairs between himself and the organization. But time and distance away from the game have given him the kind of valuable life experiences that, along with his baseball acumen, can be extremely valuable in a management position. Besides, the Phillies' assumption that Hall of Fame athletes are not suited to management has already been disproved by Bob Clarke of the Flyers and Billy Cunningham of the Sixers.

Any remaining questions about Schmidt's "aloof persona" or "inability to communicate" should be put to rest as well. Certainly, he has a much more mature perspective at the age of 50 than he had during his playing career. While he admits that he still impresses people as being "somewhat aloof," he seems now to be very approachable and willing to admit the shortcomings he had during his playing days. Perhaps the change has come, as he suggested, from "being away from the game, leading a more private life and having the humbling experience of raising two children."[2]

Mike Schmidt will always have baseball in his heart. It is hoped he will, one day, return to the game in some capacity. The Philadelphia Phillies want to build a contender, and they are calling on the wisdom of their past success for help. Why not call on the greatest player in the history of their organization?

Whatever the future holds, one thing is perfectly clear: Sometimes we don't fully appreciate what we have until it's gone. In Mike Schmidt, Philadelphia had something very special.

Notes

Chapter One

1. Tony Lucadello quoted in Mark Weingardner, *Prophet of the Sandlots: Journeys with a Major League Scout* (New York: Atlantic Monthly Press, 1990), 61.
2. *Ibid.*
3. Lucadello quoted in Jay Searcy, "Few Saw the Potential," *Philadelphia Inquirer*, June 1, 1989.
4. Stan Hochman, *Mike Schmidt: Baseball's King of Swing* (New York: Random House, 1983), 15–16.
5. Palsgrove, Galvin and Neff quoted in Paul Meyer, "Prep Honorable Mention to Series MVP," *Dayton Journal Herald*, October 23, 1980; and Hochman, 18.
6. Mike Schmidt, "Pride of the Philadelphia Phillies: An Interview with Mike Schmidt," by William C. Kashatus, *Pennsylvania Heritage* (Fall 1995): 14–15; *see also* Mike Schmidt with Barbara Walder, *Always on the Offense*, (New York: Atheneum, 1982), 22–23.
7. Interview with Mike Schmidt, October 8, 1998, Jupiter, Florida.
8. Schmidt, 24.
9. Wren quoted in Ritter Collett, "Schmidt, Pride of Dayton," *Dayton Journal Herald*, October 20, 1980.
10. Hochman, 23–24.
11. Lucadello quoted in Weingardner, 61.
12. Hochman, 25; and Frank Dolson, *Beating the Bushes: Life in the Minor Leagues* (South Bend, IN: Icarus, 1982), 125.
13. Ken Tuckey, "Phillies Win, 4–3, on Draftee's Home Run," *The Reading (PA) Times*, June 18, 1971.
14. Dolson, 125.
15. Rich Westcott and Frank Bilovsky, *The New Phillies Encyclopedia* (Philadelphia: Temple University Press, 1993), 185–86.
16. Lucadello quoted in Weingardner, 61.
17. Schmidt interview, October 8, 1998.
18. Westcott and Bilovsky, 185.
19. Schmidt interview, October 8, 1998.
20. Dolson, 10–20.
21. Schmidt quoted in Dolson, 16.
22. *Ibid.*

23. *Ibid.*, 128–29.

24. *Sporting News*, August 19, 1972.

25. Mike Schmidt, "Who's on Third.... and Why He's There," *Temple University Alumni Magazine* (December 1995), 10.

26. Hochman, 34; and Rich Westcott, *Mike Schmidt: Baseball Legend* (Philadelphia: Chelsea House, 1995), 27.

27. Schmidt quoted in Dolson, 127.

28. *Ibid.*, 130.

29. For a more comprehensive history of the Philadelphia Athletics see William C. Kashatus, *Connie Mack's '29 Triumph: The Rise and Fall of the Philadelphia Athletics Dynasty* (Jefferson, NC: McFarland, 1998).

30. Phillies history see Donald Honig, *The Philadelphia Phillies: An Illustrated History* (New York: Simon and Schuster, 1992); Allen Lewis, *The Philadelphia Phillies: A Pictorial History* (Virginia Beach: JCP, 1981); and Westcott and Bilovsky, 9–166. The best account of the 1964 debacle can be found in Dave Anderson, *Pennant Races: Baseball at Its Best* (New York: Doubleday, 1994), 255–88.

31. Westcott and Bilovsky, 484.

32. *Ibid.*, 485, 493.

33. Owens quoted in Westcott and Bilovsky, 493.

34. *Ibid.*, 133–34, 493.

35. *Ibid.*, 458–59.

36. *Ibid.*, 302.

37. *Ibid.*, 280.

38. *Ibid.*, 134; and Hochman, 43.

39. Westcott and Bilovsky, 135.

40. Ozark quoted in Ray Didinger, "He Remained in Schmidt's 'Hot Corner,'" *Philadelphia Daily News* (special feature), July 26, 1995.

41. Hochman, 49.

42. Interview with Mike Schmidt, "Michael Jack City," *The Fan* (May 1995): 27; *see also* Ray Kelly, "Schmidt's 'Strikes' Putting Crimp in Ozark Schedule," *Sporting News*, August 18, 1973; and Schmidt quoted in Westcott, 30.

43. Hochman, 39.

44. See Schmidt, "Michael Jack City," 29; and Larry Bowa with Barry Bloom, *Bleep! Larry Bowa Manages* (Chicago: Bonus Books, 1988), 161–63.

45. Schmidt quoted in George Vass, "Talent Explosion at the 'Hot Corner,'" *Baseball Digest* (May 1975), 20.

46. Schmidt quoted in Hochman, 40.

47. *Ibid.*, 40; *see also* Donna Schmidt quoted in Jay Searcy, "The Transfiguration of Mike Schmidt," *Philadelphia Inquirer Magazine*, October 26, 1986.

48. Ozark quoted in Ray Kelly, "Phils' Schmidt Rifles Shots," *Sporting News*, December 1, 1973.

49. Wine quoted in Hochman, 43.

50. Schmidt quoted in Hochman, 46.

Chapter Two

1. See Jackie Robinson, *I Never Had It Made* (New York: Putnam, 1972), 71–76; David Falkner, *Great Time Coming: The Life of Jackie Robinson from Baseball to Birmingham* (New York: Simon and Schuster, 1995), 163–64; and Tom McGrath, "Color Me Badd," *The Fan* (September 1996): 39.

2. McGrath, "Color Me Badd," 39; and Michael Sokolove, "Nice Is Not Enough," *Philadelphia Inquirer Magazine*, March 30, 1997, 21.

3. See Dick Allen and Tim Whitaker, *Crash: The Life and Times of Dick Allen* (New York: Ticknor and Fields, 1989).

4. For urban history of Philadelphia, see Edwin Wold II, *Philadelphia: Portrait of an American City* (Philadelphia: Camino Books, 1990), 320–47; and Russell F. Weigley, *Philadelphia: A 300 Year History*. (New York: W.W. Norton, 1982), 704–27.

5. See S.A. Paolantonio, *Frank Rizzo: The Last Big Man in Big City America* (Philadelphia: Camino Books, 1993).

6. See Tommy Kay, editor, *Baseball 1974* (Scottsdale, AZ: Jolast House, 1974), 71–72; and Jim Taylor, "New Life in Philly," *Baseball Digest* (November 1973), 35–38.

7. Rich Westcott and Frank Bilovsky, *The New Phillies Encyclopedia* (Philadelphia: Temple University Press, 1993), 203–04; and Mark Heisler, "Dave Cash: Key Man in Phillies' Upsurge," *Baseball Digest* (October 1974): 40–42.

8. Cash quoted in Larry Platt, "The Unloved: Mike Schmidt," *Philadelphia Magazine* (July 1995): 82.

9. *Philadelphia Inquirer*, April 4, 1974.

10. Dave Anderson, "The 'Home Run' that Raised the Roof," *New York Times*, July 2, 1974; and Ray Kelly, "Schmidt's Blast—Longest Single Ever?" *The Sporting News*, June 29, 1974.

11. Cedeño quoted in *Philadelphia Bulletin*, June 12, 1974.

12. Schmidt quoted in *Philadelphia Inquirer*, June 12, 1974.

13. Berra quoted in Stan Hochman, *Mike Schmidt: Baseball's King of Swing* (New York: Random House, 1983), 53.

14. Westcott and Bilovsky, 136.

15. Schmidt quoted in Ray Kelly, "New-style Schmidt Fires Phils' Frenzy," *The Sporting News*, June 8, 1974; and Ed Rumill, "Schmidt Finds His Other Batting Eye," *Christian Science Monitor*, June 11, 1974.

16. Schmidt, "Michael Jack City," 29; Hochman, 55–56; Schmidt quoted in Platt, 81; and Frank Dolson, *Beating the Bushes: Life in the Minor Leagues* (South Bend, IN: Icarus, 1982), 128.

17. Westcott and Bilovsky, 303. For Montañez's statistics see Rick Wolff, editor, *The Baseball Encyclopedia* (New York: Macmillan, 1990, 8th edition), 1248.

18. See Frank Dolson, "The Majors' Next Home Run King?" *Baseball Digest* (June 1974): 18–20; Pat Calabria, "Greg Luzinski: The Maturing of a Major League Slugger," *Baseball Digest* (November 1975): 45–48; For Luzinski's statistics see Wolff, 1162.

19. Larry Bowa, *Bleep! Larry Bowa Manages* (Chicago: Bonus Books, 1988), 163.

20. Schmidt quoted with Barry Bloom in Bowa, 165–66.

21. Bowa, 164.

22. Schmidt quoted in Bowa, 161.

23. Bowa, 165.

24. Schmidt quoted in Allen and Whitaker, 189.

25. Allen and Whitaker, 153.

26. *Ibid.*

27. *Ibid.*, 156–58.

28. For Allen's statistics see Wolff, 625; Barry Rosenberg, "Two for the See-Saw: Mike Schmidt and Dick Allen," *Philadelphia Magazine* (September 1975): 130–44.

29. Allen and Whitaker, 159–60.

30. Rosenberg, 138.

31. *Ibid.*, 131–32.

32. Carpenter quoted in *ibid.*, 135.

33. Ray Kelly, "Schmidt Star Still Is Rising, Phillies Assert," *The Sporting News*, February 22, 1975.

34. Schmidt quoted in Hochman, 67; and Schmidt quoted in Allen and Whitaker, 189.

35. Allen and Whitaker, 161.

36. Larry Eldridge, "Mike Schmidt Would Rather Be Consistent," *Baseball Digest* (September 1976): 68–71.

37. Ozark quoted in Rosenberg, 142.

38. Hochman, 58.

39. Schmidt quoted in Hochman, 61.

40. *Ibid.*, 59.

41. Westcott and Bilovsky, 204.

42. *Ibid.*, 137–38, 285; and Allen Lewis, "Jay Johnstone's Long Journey to Success," *Baseball Digest* (December 1976): 56–61.

43. Thomas Boswell, "Cast Offs, Stars—They Do It for the Phillies," *Washington Post*, July 15, 1976.

44. Rich Ashburn, *Philadelphia Daily News,* April 14, 1976.

45. Allen quoted in Hochman, 62.

46. *Ibid.*

47. Allen Lewis, "Schmidt Hits 4 HRs as Cubs Bow, 18–16," *Philadelphia Inquirer*, April 18, 1976.

48. McGraw quoted in *Ibid.*

49. Schmidt quoted in Hochman, 66.

50. Schmidt quoted in Larry Keith, "It's Either a Clout or an Out," *Sports Illustrated* (May 3, 1976): 22. Going into the 1976 season, Schmidt struck out once every three at-bats and homered every 15–16 at-bats.

51. Schmidt quoted in Keith, 22. Schmidt was one of the most astute students of hitting. He authored two books that focused on balancing the mental and physical aspects of the game: *Always on the Offense* with Barbara Walder (New York: Atheneum, 1982) and *The Mike Schmidt Study: Hitting Theory, Skills and Technique* with Rob Ellis (Atlanta, GA: McGriff and Bell, 1994).

52. Westcott and Bilovsky, 138.

53. Schmidt quoted in Red Smith, "The Unmaking of a Reds Fan," *New York Times*, October 9, 1976.

54. *Philadelphia Inquirer*, September 27, 1976.

55. For 1976 Phillies Statistics see Westcott and Bilovsky, 139.

56. Allen Lewis, *The Philadelphia Phillies: A Pictorial History*. (Virginia Beach: JCP, 1981), 130.

57. Allen and Whitaker, 163.

58. *Ibid.*, 164.

59. *Ibid.*, 165.

60. *Ibid.*, 166.

61. Allen and Whitaker, 167.

62. Schmidt interview, October 8, 1998, Jupiter, Florida.

63. Schmidt quoted in Allen and Whitaker, 186.

Chapter Three

1. Ray Kelly, "Schmidt's Agent Claims Million Won't Be Enough," *Philadelphia Inquirer*, December 8, 1976; "Schmidt Signs Rare Pact: Six Years for $3 Million,"

Philadelphia Inquirer, March 5, 1977; and "Modesty Plus Millions Equal Mike Schmidt," *Sporting News*, April 2, 1977. The only other players with comparable contracts were Joe Rudi of the California Angels, Don Gullett of the New York Yankees, Steve Garvey of the Los Angeles Dodgers, and Joe Morgan of the Cincinnati Reds.

2. Stan Hochman, *Mike Schmidt: Baseball's King of Swing*, (New York: Random House, 1983), 71; Barry Rosenberg, "Two for the See-Saw," *Philadelphia Magazine* (September 1975), 135–36.

3. Schmidt, "Something More," *Guideposts* (July 1987): 3.

4. Ozark quoted in Ray Kelly, "Schmidt Upset at Ozark," *Philadelphia Bulletin*, April 27, 1977.

5. Schmidt quoted in *ibid.*

6. Schmidt quoted in Frank Bilovsky, "Morganna Generous on Dad's Day," *Philadelphia Bulletin*, June 20, 1977.

7. Schmidt quoted in Si Burick, "Mike Schmidt: The Complete Ball Player," *Baseball Digest* (September 1977): 20–22.

8. Schmidt interview, October 8, 1998, Jupiter, Florida.

9. Schmidt quoted in Ray Kelly, "Schmidt Accepts Challenge—and He Pays Stiff Price," *Philadelphia Bulletin*, July 30, 1977.

10. Kison quoted in *ibid.* Schmidt finished the 1977 season with 38 home runs, 14 behind the Reds' George Foster, who captured the National League Home Run crown with 52.

11. Interview with Watson Spoelstra, April 8, 1998, Largo, Florida; *see also* Phil Elderkin, "Religion and Baseball," *Christian Science Monitor*, August 2, 1977; and Watson Spoelstra, "How 'Real Hell-Raiser' Found God," *The National Tattler* (Chicago, IL), December 8, 1974. Spoelstra was a "heavy drinker and hell-raiser" in his sportswriting days. Once president of the Baseball Writers' Association of America, he was a popular figure among sports celebrities. He became born again in 1957 as part of a bargain he made with God to care for his 18-year-old daughter, who had suffered a brain hemorrhage. When she recovered, Spoelstra quit drinking. Later, when he retired from sportswriting, he founded Baseball Chapel, gaining the official sanction of then-commissioner Bowie Kuhn.

12. *Christian Science Monitor*, August 2, 1977; and Watson Spoelstra, "Baseball Chapel: Church at the Ballpark," *1978 Cleveland Indians Scorebook*, 42; Joe Falls, "God and the Gladiators," *Parade Magazine* (April 23, 1978): 1; and Peter Becker, "At Play in the Fields of the Lord," *M Inc.* (August 1991): 74 .

13. See Randy Rieland, *Baseball in the 1970s: The New Professionals* (Alexandria, VA: Redefinition, 1989), 124–25; and Steve Mann, "The Business of Baseball," *Total Baseball*, edited by John Thorn and Pete Palmer (New York: Warner, 1989), 628–41.

14. Steve Hubbard, *Faith in Sports: Athletes and Their Religion On and Off the Field* (New York: Doubleday, 1998); "Baseball Chapel Offers Alternatives to Players," *San Francisco Chronicle*, August 14, 1990. For accounts of other Christian athletes and their conversions, see Dave Branon and Joe Pellegrino, *Safe at Home: Winning Players Talk About Baseball and Their Faith* (Chicago: Moody Press, 1992).

15. Other major league teams that had a strong Christian influence during the 1970s and 1980s were the California Angels, Los Angeles Dodgers, Montreal Expos, New York Mets, Philadelphia Phillies, Pittsburgh Pirates, San Francisco Giants and Texas Rangers.

16. Schmidt interview, October 8, 1998.

17. Harry Hecht, "Jim Kaat: The Majors' Geriatric Wonder," *Baseball Digest* (October 1978): 81–83.

18. Ray Didinger, "Garry Maddox: The Man with the Golden Glove," *Baseball Digest* (September 1978): 50–54; and Phil Elderkin, "Garry Maddox: The Phils' Premier Ball Hawk," *Baseball Digest* (August 1979): 68–70.

19. Schmidt interview, October 8, 1998.

20. Schmidt quoted in Skip Myslenski, "Mike Schmidt: It's Just a Question of Mind Over Batter," *Boston Globe*, July 10, 1977.

21. Allen Lewis, *The Philadelphia Phillies: A Pictorial History* (Virginia Beach, VA: JCP, 1981), 132.

22. Donald Honig, *The Philadelphia Phillies: An Illustrated History* (New York: Simon and Schuster, 1992), 203.

23. *Ibid.*, 207.

24. Lewis, 207–09.

25. Schmidt, "Something More," 3.

26. *Ibid.*, 4.

27. *Ibid.*

28. Donna Schmidt quoted in Jay Searcy, "The Transfiguration of Mike Schmidt," *Philadelphia Inquirer Magazine*, October 26, 1986, 8.

29. Schmidt interview: October 8, 1998; Schmidt, "Something More," 4; and Schmidt, "Pride of the Philadelphia Phillies: An Interview with Mike Schmidt," by William C. Kashatus, *Pennsylvania Heritage* (Fall 1995): 16.

30. Schmidt quoted in Rich Ashburn, "Schmidt: Boo-birds are on target," *Philadelphia Bulletin*, August 20, 1978; and Schmidt, "Pride of the Philadelphia Phillies," 16.

31. Donna Schmidt quoted in Hochman, 61–62.

32. Kempton quoted in Schmidt, "Something More," 5.

33. Schmidt interview, October 8, 1998.

34. Chris Smith, "God Is an .800 Hitter," *New York Times Magazine* (July 27, 1997), 27–28; George Vecsey, "Religion Becomes an Important Part of the Baseball Scene," *New York Times*, May 10, 1981; Rieland, 43; and Hubbard, 41. In the most critical series of articles, appearing in *Sports Illustrated* in 1976, Frank Deford wrote, "In the final analysis, sport has had a greater impact upon religion than the other way around. While athletics does not appear to have been improved by the religious blitzkrieg, the religious people who work that side of the street seem to have been colored by some of the worst attitudes found in sport. The temper of the athletic religion is competitive, full of coaches and cheerleaders, with an overriding sense of wins and losses, stars and recruiting, game plans, and dugout chatter." See Deford, "Religion in Sports," *Sports Illustrated*, April 19, 26, and May 3, 1976.

35. Schmidt, "Something More," 5; Schmidt, "Pride of the Philadelphia Phillies," 16; and Hochman, 76.

36. Rich Westcott and Frank Bilovsky, *The New Phillies Encyclopedia* (Philadelphia: Temple University Press, 1993) 141; and Honig, 209–11.

37. Schmidt interview, October 8, 1998; and Schmidt, "Something More," 5.

38. See UPI, "Schmidt, Johnstone Make 'All-Cool' Team," *Philadelphia Bulletin*, August 11, 1975.

39. For further information on Christian ethics see Richard J. Foster, *The Challenge of the Disciplined Life* (New York: Harper, 1985); and Arnold D. Hunt, et al., "Christianity," in *Ethics of World Religions* (San Diego, CA: Greenhaven, 1991), 45–82. For further information on how Christian ethics applies to athletes, see Hubbard.

40. "Schmidt No Stranger to Golf or Community Service," *Philadelphia Inquirer*, July 2, 1992.

Chapter Four

1. Rich Westcott and Frank Bilovsky, *The New Phillies Encyclopedia* (Philadelphia: Temple University Press, 1993), 492–93.

2. Allen Lewis, *The Philadelphia Phillies: A Pictorial History* (Virginia Beach: JCP, 1981), 145.

3. Pete Rose and Roger Kahn, *Pete Rose: My Story* (New York: MacMillan, 1989), 9–10.

4. See Mark Whicker, "'Old' Rose Is Forever Young," *Philadelphia Bulletin*, October 14, 1980; Rose quoted in Thomas Boswell, "For Rose, Nearly 40, Series Could Be the Last Hurrah," *Washington Post*, October 19, 1980; and Stan Hochman, *Mike Schmidt: Baseball's King of Swing* (New York: Random House, 1983), 13, 80–82.

5. Donald Honig, *The Philadelphia Phillies: An Illustrated History* (New York, Simon and Schuster, 1992), 212; Lewis, 145. To make the signing of Rose possible, Bill Giles, the Phillies' executive vice-president, appealed to the TV station that carried the Phillies' games. The station agreed to pay the Phillies $600,000 more for the TV rights if Rose was signed by the team. Ticket sales also skyrocketed. The Phillies sold more than three million tickets in 1979, helping them to defray some of the cost of Rose's salary.

6. Stewart Wolpin, "Pete Rose," *The Ball Players: Baseball's Ultimate Reference Book*, edited by Mike Shatzkin (New York: William Morrow, 1990), 937–38.

7. Schmidt quoted in Paul Dickson, *Baseball's Greatest Quotations* (New York: Edward Burlingame, 1991), 386.

8. Hochman, 18.

9. Schmidt quoted in Ray Kelly, "Move Schmidt? 'No Way' says Ozark," *Sporting News*, November 25, 1978.

10. Schmidt, "Pride of the Philadelphia Phillies: An Interview with Mike Schmidt," by William C. Kashatus, *Pennsylvania Heritage* (Fall 1995): 14–15.

11. Lewis, 147; and Honig, 213–14.

12. Westcott and Bilovsky, 459–60; Tom Jozwik, "Dallas Green," *The Ball Players*, 409; and Lewis, 147.

13. Schmidt quoted in Hochman, 85.

14. Westcott and Bilovsky, 143, 325.

15. Mike Schmidt, with Barbara Walder, *Always on the Offense* (New York:Athenewn, 1982), 55–57.

16. Rose quoted in Michael V. Sokolove, *Hustle: The Myth, Life and Lies of Pete Rose* (New York: Simon and Schuster, 1990), 227.

17. Rose quoted in Hochman, 92.

18. *Sports Illustrated*, April 10, 1980.

19. Honig, 213–14; Lewis, 148; and Schmidt quoted in Hochman, 84.

20. Dallas Green quoted in Hochman, 184.

21. Honig, 215; and Lewis, 148–49.

22. *Trenton (N.J.) Times*, July 8, 1980.

23. David Q. Voigt, *American Baseball: From Postwar Expansion to the Electronic Age* (University Park, PA: Pennsylvania State University Press, 1983), 260–61.

24. David Q. Voigt, "The History of Major League Baseball," *Total Baseball*, edited by John Thorn and Pete Palmer (New York: Warner, 1989), 47. In 1983, three Kansas City Royals were sentenced to jail terms as convicted users, and a Dodger pitcher was suspended. In 1985, a San Diego Padres player was traded because of drug abuse. Most damaging, however, were revelations coming from two Pittsburgh court

cases of 17 players who abused drugs. Baseball commissioner Peter Ueberroth's attempt to force all players to submit to periodic drug testing was blocked by the Players' Association, which insisted that the issue be addressed through collective bargaining. Undaunted, Ueberoth suspended the accused players from the game and required each one to donate up to 10 percent of his salary to charity and to participate in anti-drug campaigns as a prerequisite for reinstatement.

25. See Carpenter and Yatron quoted in Hal Bodley, "Angry Phils Deny Drug Report," *Sporting News*, July 26, 1980.

26. Schmidt quoted in *ibid*.

27. Honig, 215; Lewis, 149–50.

28. Owens quoted in Westcott and Bilovsky, 492.

29. Schmidt, *Always on the Offense*, 178–79.

30. Lewis, 150–52; Westcott and Bilovsky, 145; and Steve Wulf, "Dilly of a Win for Philly," *Sports Illustrated*, October 13, 1980.

31. For Phillies 1980 statistics see Rick Wolff, editor, *The Baseball Encyclopedia* (New York: Macmillan, 1990, 8th edition), 480; also Honig, 216.

32. For Houston Astros 1980 statistics see Wolff, 481.

33. *Philadelphia Inquirer*, October 8, 1980; and Ron Fimrite, "Wow, What a Playoff," *Sports Illustrated*, October 20, 1980.

34. *Philadelphia Inquirer*, October 9, 1980; and Fimrite, "Wow."

35. *Philadelphia Inquirer*, October 11, 1980; and Fimrite, "Wow."

36. Rose quoted in *Philadelphia Bulletin*, October 12, 1980.

37. *Philadelphia Bulletin*, October 12, 1980; Fimrite, "Wow."

38. Schmidt quoted in Bob Ibach and Tim Panaccio, *The Comeback Kids: 1980 World Series Flashback* (Bel Air, CA: Bel Air Printing, 1980), 10; and Schmidt quoted in Philadelphia Daily News, October 16, 1980.

39. *Philadelphia Inquirer*, October 13, 1980; and Fimrite, "Wow."

40. Ruly Carpenter quoted in Larry Eichel, "The Happy End to a Long Ordeal," *Philadelphia Inquirer*, October 13, 1980.

41. Schmidt, *Always on the Offense*, 179–80.

42. For 1980 Kansas City Royals Statistics see Wolff, 484, 2728.

43. *Philadelphia Inquirer*, October 15, 1980; and Ron Fimrite, "One Heart Stopper After Another," *Sports Illustrated*, October 27, 1980; Gene Schoor, *The History of the World Series* (New York: William Morrow, 1990), 344.

44. Schmidt quoted in *Philadelphia Daily News*, October 16, 1980.

45. *Philadelphia Inquirer*, October 16, 1980; Fimrite, "One Heart Stopper."

46. George Brett quoted in Ibach and Panaccio, 8.

47. Schmidt quoted in Danny Robbins, "Leaving 8 on Base, Schmidt Can Only Welcome New Day," *Philadelphia Inquirer*, October 19, 1980.

48. Fimrite, One Heart Stopper," 29; Ibach and Panaccio, 9.

49. Schmidt quoted in Jayson Stark, "Unser, Schmidt Key Win," *Philadelphia Inquirer*, October 20, 1980.

50. *Ibid.*

51. Schmidt quoted in Ibach and Panaccio, 10.

52. *Philadelphia Bulletin*, October 22, 1980; *Philadelphia Inquirer*, October 22, 1980; Lewis, 168–71; Ibach and Panaccio, 7–8; and Schoor, 346–47.

53. Schmidt, *Always on the Offense*, 177.

54. Schmidt, "Pride of the Philadelphia Phillies," 17.

55. McGraw quoted in Ibach and Panaccio, 1.

56. Schmidt quoted in *Ibid.*

57. Pete Axthelm gave a very different interpretation of the Phillies' relationship

with their fans and the press in his article, "Those Malevolent Phillies," which appeared in the November 3, 1980, issue of *Newsweek*. Axthelm stated that the "police attack dogs who snarled at the Phillies' fans from the carpeted field were aimed in the wrong direction." He suggested that they would have done better to attack the "malevolent Phillies," especially Larry Bowa, who "sneered that the boos of the fans inspired him"; Lonnie Smith, who "led a few teammates in obscene chants directed at the press"; and Steve Carlton, who "withdrew in sullen splendor to the off-limits trainer's room while the reporters maintained their demeaning vigil outside the door of the sanctuary."

58. Schmidt, *Always on the Offense*, 29.

59. Schmidt quoted in *Ibid.*, 177; and *Philadelphia Inquirer*, November 12, 1980.

60. Larry Bowa with Larry Bloom, *Bleep! Larry Bowa Manages* (Chicago: Bonus Books, 1988), 264.

61. Frank Dolson, "MVP Mike: Schmidt Flattered at Unanimous Vote by Writers," *Philadelphia Inquirer*, November 27, 1980.

62. Schmidt quoted in *ibid.*

63. Schmidt quoted in Hal Bodley, "Schmidt's Burning Desire: MVP," *The Sporting News*, October 18, 1980; *See also* Ted Silary, "When It Came to Chores, Mike Could Do It All," *Philadelphia Daily News* (Special Report: "Legends in Their Own Time"), July 26, 1995.

64. Schmidt quoted in Bodley.

Chapter Five

1. Steve Wulf, "National League East: Scouting Report," *Sports Illustrated* (April 13, 1981): 36–37.

2. See Randy Rieland, *Baseball in the 1970s: The New Professionals* (Alexandria, VA: Redefinition, 1989), 124–25; and Steve Mann, "The Business of Baseball," *Total Baseball*, edited by John Thorn and Pete Palmer (New York: Warner, 1989), 628–41.

3. David Q. Voigt, *American Baseball: From Postwar Expansion to Electronic Age* (University Park, PA: Pennsylvania State University Press, 1983), 336–37. Marvin Miller, a labor economist for the United States Steel Workers of America, was made the executive director of the Players' Association in 1966. A genius in labor relations, he reshaped the structure of the Association from a passive vehicle that was frequently exploited by the owners to a powerful labor union. He used federal laws to force the owners to negotiate formal contracts known as the "Basic Agreement." These spelled out working conditions, minimum salary and pensions. While the players hailed Miller as a "Great Emancipator," the owners viewed him as the major obstacle in player negotiations.

4. *Ibid.*, 346–47. Originally, the players planned to strike on May 29, but postponed when a National Labor Relations Board Council filed an unfair labor practice suit against the owners. Their hope for a settlement vanished when a federal court disallowed the petition.

5. Schmidt quoted in Stan Hochman, *Mike Schmidt: Baseball's King of Swing* (New York: Random House, 1983), 114.

6. Voigt, 348.

7. *Ibid.*, 348–49. Under the fifth basic agreement, players' pensions and reentry draft rights were not penalized because of time lost due to the strike. They were

also given a week's time to get back into playing condition. The new agreement extended through the end of the 1984 season and provided major league baseball with three full seasons of relief from labor turmoil.

8. *Ibid.*, 348.

9. Hochman, 117–118; and Rich Westcott and Frank Bilovsky, *The New Phillies Encyclopedia* (Philadelphia: Temple University Press, 1993), 146–47.

10. Green quoted in Hochman, 118.

11. Hochman, 87; *see also* Schmidt quoted in Jim Kaplan, "Third Is the Word," *Sports Illustrated* (April 13, 1981): 23–24.

12. Westcott and Bilovsky, 460.

13. *Ibid.*, 460–61.

14. Carpenter quoted in *ibid.*, 485.

15. *Ibid.*, 485.

16. *Ibid.*, 485–86.

17. Schmidt quoted in *Philadelphia Bulletin*, November 18, 1981.

18. Chuck Newman, "Phils' Third Baseman Wins His Second MVP," *Philadelphia Inquirer*, November 18, 1981; and Gerry Fraley, "2d MVP for Mike: Time to Talk Money," *Philadelphia Bulletin*, November 18, 1981. In winning his second straight MVP Award, Schmidt joined National Leaguers Ernie Banks of the Chicago Cubs (1958–59) and Joe Morgan of the Cincinnati Reds (1975–76). In the American League, those who won back-to-back MVPs were Jimmie Foxx of the Philadelphia Athletics (1932–33); Hal Newhouser of the Detroit Tigers (1944–45); and New York Yankees Yogi Berra (1954–55), Mickey Mantle (1956–57) and Roger Maris (1960–61).

19. Voigt, 228.

20. Steve Mann, "The Business of Baseball," in *Total Baseball*, edited by Pete Palmer and John Thorn (New York: Warner, 1989), 636.

21. *Ibid.* Few players were hurt by signing multiyear contracts. But among the victims were Hall of Famers Johnny Bench and Tom Seaver, who missed out on millions by agreeing to long-term deals early in the free agent era, before salaries skyrocketed.

22. Rosenberg quoted in Ben Yagoda, "What's the Big Deal?" *Philly Sport* (July 1989): 33.

23. Schmidt quoted in *ibid.*

24. *Ibid.*, 32.

25. Rosenberg quoted in *Philadelphia Bulletin*, November 18, 1981.

26. Bill Conlin, "Most Valuable ($10 M) Player," *Philadelphia Daily News*, December 22, 1981.

27. Giles quoted in *ibid.*

28. *Ibid.*

29. Schmidt quoted in Frank Dolson, "Phils' 6-year Pact Makes Schmidt NL's Richest Player," *Philadelphia Inquirer*, December 22, 1981.

30. Schmidt quoted in Ray Didinger, "Look What They've Done to Our Game," *Philadelphia Daily News* (Special Section), July 26, 1995.

Chapter Six

1. Mike Schmidt, "Pride of the Philadelphia Phillies: An Interview with Mike Schmidt," by William C. Kashatus, *Pennsylvania Heritage* (Fall 1995), 16.

2. See E. Digby Baltzell, *Puritan Boston and Quaker Philadelphia* (New York:

Free Press, 1979). Baltzell argued that Philadelphia Quakers were "too egalitarian" and "too content to rest on their inherited wealth and privileges" to provide effective leadership. In comparison to Boston's Brahmins, who he felt exemplified the Protestant work ethic, Baltzell saw the Quakers as inferior, failing to instill "a strong desire and capacity to take the lead in both community building and community reform." These failures are traced to the Quaker theology, which promoted both anti-authoritarianism and an exceptionally progressive view of equality.

3. See Frederick G. Lieb, *Connie Mack: Grand Old Man of Baseball* (New York: G.P. Putnam's Sons, 1945); and William C. Kashatus, *Connie Mack's '29 Triumph: The Rise and Fall of the Philadelphia Athletics Dynasty* (Jefferson, NC: McFarland, 1998).

4. Rich Westcott and Frank Bilovsky, *The New Phillies Encyclopedia* (Philadelphia: Temple University Press, 1993), 47–48.

5. Mark Bowden, "The Short, Sad Spring of Michael Schmidt," *Philadelphia Inquirer Magazine*, May 16, 1982.

6. Frank Dolson, "Schmidt Fights to Stay on Top," *Philadelphia Inquirer*, June 3, 1982.

7. Pat Corrales quoted in Jayson Stark, "Phils Wait for the Power in Schmidt's Bat to Resurface," *Philadelphia Inquirer*, July 4, 1982.

8. Stan Hochman, *Mike Schmidt: Baseball's King of Swing* (New York: Random House, 1983), 123–24.

9. Pete Rose quoted in *ibid.*, 125.

10. Schmidt quoted in *ibid.*, 126.

11. Schmidt quoted in "Schmidt Examines Unhappy Season," *New York Times*, October 3, 1982.

12. Westcott and Bilovsky, 148, 251–52. Hayes' most productive year with the Phillies came in 1986, when he hit .305 and collected 19 home runs and 98 RBI. He didn't come close to hitting .300 again, finishing his nine-year, Phillies career with a .267 average.

13. *Ibid.*, 149.

14. Steve Wulf, "In Philadelphia, They're the Wheeze Kids," *Sports Illustrated* (March 14, 1983): 26.

15. *Ibid.*, 27–28.

16. Steve Wulf, "Philly Is Streaking for Home," *Sports Illustrated* (October 3, 1983): 20–25.

17. Hal Bodley, "Phillies' Schmidt Should Stop Thinking About Slump," *USA Today*, June 6, 1983; and Frank Dolson, "The Trials of '83 Could Not Keep Schmidt Down," *Philadelphia Inquirer*, October 4, 1983.

18. See Peter Pascarelli's daily columns in the *Philadelphia Inquirer* during the periods May 11 to June 6 and July 14 to August 30, 1983. Quote is taken from Pascarelli, "Phillies Need a Mr. September," *Philadelphia Inquirer*, August 21, 1983.

19. Schmidt quoted in Dolson, "Trials of '83."

20. Schmidt quoted in Ralph Bernstein, "Schmidt Lashes Out at Management," *New York Times*, September 9, 1983; and Bill Fleischman, "The Weight of Philly on His Shoulders," *Inside Sports* (June 1984): 22.

21. Paul Owens quoted in *ibid.*

22. Westcott and Bilovsky, 150.

23. *Ibid.*, 631–33; and Ron Fimrite, "The Old and the Relentless Beat the Young and the Restless," *Sports Illustrated* (October 17, 1983): 18–20.

24. See Rick Wolff, editor, *The Baseball Encyclopedia* (New York: MacMillan, 1990, 8th edition), 501.

25. Peter Pascarelli, "Maddox's Homer Beats Orioles," *Philadelphia Inquirer*, October 12, 1983.

26. Peter Pascarelli, "O's Even Series on 4–1 Win," *Philadelphia Inquirer*, October 13, 1983.

27. Eddie Murray quoted in Al Morganti, "When a Power Hitter Doesn't Hit," *Philadelphia Inquirer*, October 14, 1983.

28. Paul Owens quoted in Peter Pascarelli, "Rose Is Benched in Surprise Move," *Philadelphia Inquirer*, October 15, 1983.

29. Pete Rose quoted in Frank Dolson, "Unexpected Move Stuns and Embarrasses Rose," *Philadelphia Inquirer*, October 15, 1983.

30. Peter Pascarelli, "O's Take Lead in Series on 3–2 Win," *Philadelphia Inquirer*, October 15, 1983.

31. Schmidt quoted in Frank Dolson, "Schmidt Toughs Out the Pressures of a Slump," *Philadelphia Inquirer*, October 6, 1983.

32. Steve Wulf, "The Orioles All Pitched In," *Sports Illustrated* (October 24, 1983): 24–28.

33. Pete Rose quoted in "Release 'the best thing' for Rose; Sure He'll Find Another Team," *Philadelphia Bulletin*, October 20, 1983. Rose rejected the role of a part-time player with the Phillies because he was just 201 hits short of breaking Ty Cobb's all-time career major league hit record of 4,191. Rose eventually broke the record when he returned to the Cincinnati Reds as a player-manager.

34. Schmidt quoted in Jayson Stark, "For Rose, Retirement Is Out, But So Is His Future with Phils," *Philadelphia Inquirer*, October 17, 1983.

35. Schmidt quoted in Fleischman, 24.

36. Schmidt quoted in Hochman, 130.

37. Schmidt, "Pride of Phillies," 19.

38. Fleischman, 25.

39. Schmidt quoted in *Los Angeles Times*, March 31, 1975; *see also* Schmidt quotations in Peter Pascarelli, "The Thinking Man's Superstar," *Sporting News*, June 11, 1984; and John Lowe, "Home Sweet Home: Not for Schmidt," *Dodger Blue*, June 15, 1984.

40. Frank Dolson, "Schmidt Home Run Lifts Phils in Vet Debut," *Philadelphia Inquirer*, April 11, 1984.

41. Bill Giles quoted in Fleischman, 25.

42. Pete Rose cited in *ibid*.

43. Schmidt quoted in Hochman, 112; *see also* Schmidt quotations in Bob Ibach and Tim Panaccio, *Comeback Kids: 1980 World Series Flashback* (Bel Air Printing, 1980), 11; and Schmidt, *Always on the Offense*, 29.

44. Fleischman, 24.

45. *Ibid*.

46. Schmidt quoted in Peter Hadekel, "Interview," *Montreal Gazette*, June 29, 1985.

47. Schmidt quoted in Peter Pascarelli, "Schmidt Hits the Fans as Being 'beyond help," *Philadelphia Inquirer*, June 30, 1985; *see also* Schmidt quoted in Pascarelli, "New Target: Schmidt Now Focuses His Ire on Media Instead of Phillies' Fans," *Philadelphia Inquirer*, July 1, 1985.

48. *Ibid*.

49. Frank Dolson, "A Bewigged Schmidt Tries to Repair the Hurt," *Philadelphia Inquirer*, July 2, 1985.

50. Schmidt quoted in Frank Dolson, "Trials of '83."

51. Westcott and Bilovsky, 151–53.

52. Peter Pascarelli, "It's Official: Schmidt Moving to First," *Philadelphia Inquirer*, May 28, 1985.

53. Schmidt quoted in *ibid.*
54. Schmidt quoted in Peter Pascarelli, "Behind the Schmidt Move, Logic," *Philadelphia Inquirer*, May 28, 1985.
55. *Ibid.*
56. Schmidt quoted in Joseph Durso, "Schmidt, Guerrero Turned It Around," *New York Times*, September 3, 1985; and Jayson Stark, "Considering Life Without Schmidt," *Philadelphia Inquirer*, October 5, 1986.
57. Gary Carter and Keith Hernandez quoted in Thomas Rogers, "Schmidt Joins an Elite Club with Third MVP Award," *New York Times*, November 20, 1986.
58. Schmidt quoted in Peter Pascarelli, "Schmidt Is National League MVP," *Philadelphia Inquirer*, November 20, 1986.
59. Schmidt quoted in Stan Hochman, "Planning for the Future," *Philadelphia Daily News*, November 20, 1986.
60. Schmidt quoted in Jay Searcy, "The Transformation of Mike Schmidt," *Philadelphia Inquirer Magazine*, October 26, 1986.

Chapter Seven

1. Peter Pascarelli, "Mike Schmidt: Staying Power," *Sporting News* (March 30, 1987): 12.
2. Schmidt quoted in Stan Hochman, "Schmidt Critical of Phillies," *Philadelphia Daily News*, May 16, 1987.
3. Larry Bowa with Barry Bloom, *Bleep! Larry Bowa Manages* (Chicago: Bonus Books, 1988), 161–62.
4. Schmidt quoted in Jayson Stark, "Considering Life Without Schmidt," *Philadelphia Inquirer*, October 5, 1986; Stan Hochman, "Planning for the Future," *Philadelphia Daily News*, November 20, 1986; and Peter Pascarelli, "Schmidt Might Have Eye on Front Office Post," *Philadelphia Inquirer*, November 20, 1986.
5. Schmidt quoted in Peter Pascarelli, "At Long Last, Philadelphia Fans Appreciate Their Cerebral Slugger," *Sporting News 1987 Baseball Yearbook*, 24; and Schmidt quoted in Stark, "Considering Life Without Schmidt."
6. Schmidt quoted in "Schmidt Counts Years Past, One Left," *Philadelphia Inquirer*, September 27, 1986.
7. Schmidt quoted in Peter Pascarelli, "Schmidt Is NY MVP," *Philadelphia Inquirer*, November 20, 1986.
8. Donna Schmidt quoted in Marc Schogol, "For Phillies' Wives, Sometimes Its Foul," *Philadelphia Inquirer*, June 12, 1988.
9. *Ibid.*
10. *Ibid.*
11. *Ibid.*
12. Schmidt quoted in Pascarelli, "At Long Last."
13. Ben Yagoda, "What's the Big Deal?" *Philly Sport* (July 1989): 33–34. Rosenberg and his staff handle every aspect of their client's financial needs. Schmidt's paycheck went directly to Arthur Rosenberg and Associates. Subsequently, a small amount was deposited into Schmidt's checking account for daily expenses. Rosenberg and Associates paid all bills, did all the taxes, arranged insurance and legal representation, and also handled investments. Rosenberg and Associates' investment strategy is a conservative one. Seventy percent of assets are invested in short-term interest-rate-sensitive investments such as CDs and money markets. Another 20 percent in equity,

such as stocks. The remaining ten percent is invested in real estate and private ventures. Schmidt paid a monthly fee for these services.

14. Bill Giles quoted in Stark, "Considering Life Without Schmidt"; and Giles quoted in Frank Dolson, "The Glory, the Pain of His Day," *Philadelphia Inquirer*, November 20, 1986.

15. Schmidt quoted in Pascarelli, "Staying Power," 12.

16. "Schmidt's Home Run Statistics," *Phillies 1987 Media Guide* (Philadelphia: Philadelphia Phillies, 1987), 70–75.

17. Mike Schmidt, "Pride of the Philadelphia Phillies: An Interview with Mike Schmidt," by William C. Kashatus, *Pennsylvania Heritage* (Fall 1995): 16.

18. Mark Bowden, "The Short, Sad Spring of Schmidt," *Philadelphia Inquirer Magazine*, May 16, 1982.

19. Schmidt quoted in Rod Beaton, "Schmidt Counting Ws Not HRs," *USA Today*, April 17, 1987.

20. Peter Pascarelli, "Phillies Win, 6–2; 499th for Schmidt," *Philadelphia Inquirer*, April 18, 1987.

21. Donna Schmidt quoted in "Sometimes It's Foul"; and Frank Dolson, "A Real Life Hero," *Philadelphia Inquirer*, June 2, 1989.

22. Schmidt quoted in Jayson Stark, "Schmidt Slugs His 500th and Gives Phils a Victory," *Philadelphia Inquirer*, April 19, 1987.

23. *Ibid.*

24. Harry Kalas quoted in *Ibid.*

25. Jim Leyland quoted in Dolson, "A Real-Life Hero."

26. Schmidt quoted in Frank Dolson, "Schmidt's 500th Came Against a Worthy Opponent," *Philadelphia Inquirer*, April 19, 1987.

27. Schmidt quoted in Stark, "Schmidt Slugs 500th"; *See also* Rich Westcott and Frank Bilovsky, "Mike Schmidt Hits His 500th Home Run," *The New Phillies Encyclopedia* (Philadelphia: Temple University Press, 1993), 565.

28. "Schmidt Starts Charity Drive," *Philadelphia Inquirer*, April 18, 1987.

29. See National Institute on Drug Abuse, "Mike Schmidt on Cocaine Abuse," (Washington DC: Department of Health and Human Services, 1987).

30. Rick Sutcliffe quoted in Frank Dolson, "Even His Opponents Want to See No. 500," *Philadelphia Inquirer*, April 17, 1987.

31. *Ibid.*

32. Shane Rawley, "Michael Jack Schmidt," *1987 Phillies Yearbook*.

33. *Ibid.*

34. Schmidt quoted in Stark, "Considering Life Without Schmidt."

35. Jayson Stark, "Schmidt Crushes Expos," *Philadelphia Inquirer*, June 15, 1987.

36. Westcott and Bilovsky, 155–56; and Sam Carchidi, "Schmidt Is Thrilled to Add to His List of All-Star Starts," *Philadelphia Inquirer*, July 9, 1987.

37. Westcott and Bilovsky, 155–56.

38. Jayson Stark, "Phils Get Schmidt for 2 More," *Philadelphia Inquirer*, November 11, 1987.

39. Bill Giles quoted in Frank Dolson, "Old Pro May Try a New Attitude," *Philadelphia Inquirer*, November 11, 1987.

40. John Felske quoted in Angelo Cataldi, "Phils Look for Their Leader and Find Only Their Star," *Philadelphia Inquirer*, May 29, 1988.

41. Schmidt quoted in Dolson, "Old Pro, New Attitude."

42. Jayson Stark, "Elia Considering Moving Schmidt to First Base," *Philadelphia Inquirer*, July 10, 1988.

43. Schmidt quoted in Cataldi, "Phils Look for Their Leader."

44. Bruce Buschel, "Even Superstars Get the Blues," *Philly Sport* (June/July 1988).

45. See two exemplary articles that appeared during the nadir of Schmidt's slump in 1988: Bill Lyon, "He's Entitled to His Slump," *Philadelphia Inquirer*, July 9, 1988; and Frank Dolson, "A Hitter's Quest to Regain His Lost Stroke," *Philadelphia Inquirer*, July 10, 1988.

46. Westcott and Bilovsky, 157–58, 495–96.

47. Schmidt quoted in Frank Dolson, "Schmidt Says Injury Won't Threaten Career," *Philadelphia Inquirer*, August 28, 1988; *see also* Peter Pascarelli, "Schmidt Has a Tear in Rotator Cuff," *Philadelphia Inquirer*, August 27, 1988; and Sam Carchidi, "Schmidt Tear Is Complete, But Small," *Philadelphia Inquirer*, August 31, 1988.

48. Jay Searcy, "Schmidt Is an Issue and He Won't Duck It," *Philadelphia Inquirer*, September 4, 1988; Jayson Stark, "Schmidt Has Surgery; Future with Phils Uncertain," *Philadelphia Inquirer*, September 8, 1988.

49. Schmidt quoted in Jayson Stark, "Mike Schmidt's View From a Hospital Room," *Philadelphia Inquirer*, September 9, 1988.

50. Diane Pucin, "Schmidt Is a Free Agent," *Philadelphia Inquirer*, October 22, 1988.

51. Bill Madden, "Yankees Plan to Make Bid for Schmidt," *New York Daily News*, October 25, 1988.

52. Peter Pascarelli, "For the Phillies, the Off-Season Is Where the Action Is," *Philadelphia Inquirer*, October 30, 1988; and Frank Dolson, "Rose's Dream Was Only That," *Philadelphia Inquirer*, March 1, 1989.

53. Paul Hagen, "Schmidt Takes First Step," *Philadelphia Daily News*, December 8, 1988; Peter Pascarelli, "Phils Sign Schmidt to 1-Year Pact," *Philadelphia Inquirer*, December 8, 1988.

54. Schmidt quoted in Jayson Stark, "A Smile After Months of Doubt," *Philadelphia Inquirer*, December 8, 1988.

55. *Ibid.*

56. Frank Dolson, "First Base Would Be Just Perfect for Schmidt but ..." *Philadelphia Inquirer*, February 22, 1989.

57. Lee Thomas quoted in Peter Pascarelli, "Schmidt to Start at 3rd Base, but with Question Marks," *Philadelphia Inquirer*, March 31, 1989.

58. Nick Leyva quoted in *ibid.*

59. Schmidt quoted by Jay Searcy, "Mike Schmidt Says the Season for Holding Back Is Past," *Philadelphia Inquirer*, April 2, 1989.

60. Peter Pascarelli, "Giants Deal Phils Fifth Loss in Row," *Philadelphia Inquirer*, May 29, 1989; also Westcott and Bilovsky, 158.

61. Excerpts from Schmidt's statement appeared in *Philadelphia Inquirer*, May 30, 1989; *see also* Peter Pascarelli, "Schmidt's Career Ends with Tears," *Philadelphia Inquirer*, May 30, 1989; Frank Dolson, "Departure Brings Tears, but Memories Bring Joy," *Philadelphia Inquirer*, May 30, 1989.

62. Bill Giles quoted in *ibid.*

63. Schmidt quoted in Bill Conlin, "Schmidt's Heart Does His Talking," *Philadelphia Daily News*, May 31, 1989.

64. *Ibid.*

65. Schmidt quoted in Bill Lyon, "A Night of Cheers, More Tears," *Philadelphia Inquirer*, June 4, 1989.

66. Schmidt quoted in Jayson Stark, "Schmidt Reflects on Last Showcase," *Philadelphia Inquirer*, July 12, 1989; *see also* Peter Pascarelli, "Retired Star Is Gratified," *Philadelphia Inquirer*, July 6, 1989; and Mike Dodd, "Schmidt Voted All-Star Berth,"

USA Today, July 6, 1989. Chris Sabo of the Cincinnati Reds, the runner-up to Schmidt in the All-Star voting, started at third base.

67. Bill Brown, "Nobody Did It Better: Schmidt Selected TSN Player of the Decade," *The Sporting News*, January 29, 1990.

68. Frank Dolson, "Deep Feelings Warms Night for Schmidt," *Philadelphia Inquirer*, May 27, 1990.

69. Bill Giles quoted in Ray Didinger, "Schmidt Trying to Connect: Phil's Rebuffs Take the Glow Out of Retirement," *Philadelphia Daily News*, May 29, 1991.

70. *Ibid.*

71. Schmidt quoted in Didinger, "Schmidt Trying to Connect."

72. *Ibid.*

73. Dr. Joel Fish quoted in Stephen Rush, "From Baseball to Business," *Nation's Business* (October 1996): 50.

74. See Jay Searcy, "Schmidt Moves Behind the Mike," *Philadelphia Inquirer*, April 15, 1990; and Lee Winfrey, "The Phils' No. 20 Behind the Mike," *Philadelphia Inquirer's TV Week*, May 20–26, 1990.

75. Jayson Stark, "Schmidt: The Phillies 'know where to find me'," *Philadelphia Inquirer*, January 30, 1993.

76. See Glen Macnow and Timothy Dwyer, "Schmidt–PNI Golf Tournament Was Unable to Deliver to Charity," *Philadelphia Inquirer*, February 25, 1993; Timothy Dwyer and Jayson Stark, "Schmidt Says Charity Agreed to Wait," *Philadelphia Inquirer*, February 26, 1993; Timothy Dwyer and Robert Zausner, "Charity to Remain with Golf Tourney," *Philadelphia Inquirer*, March 12, 1993; and Timothy Dwyer and Michael Bamberger, "Charity Golf Event Promised Too Much," *Philadelphia Inquirer*, May 17, 1993.

77. Schmidt quoted in Jayson Stark, "Time a Cruel Foe for 2 Great Phils," *Philadelphia Inquirer*, February 10, 1991.

Chapter Eight

1. See George B. Kirsch, "Bats, Balls, and Bullets: Baseball and the Civil War," *Civil War Times Illustrated* (May 1998): 30–37; and National Baseball Hall of Fame and Museum, *1995 Yearbook* (Cooperstown, NY: National Baseball Hall of Fame and Museum, 1995), 4, 10. Legend has it that one summer afternoon in 1839, Abner Doubleday chased the cows off a local pasture and organized a game that has come to be known as our national pastime. Inspired by the folklore, a small group of former baseball players, politicians, and businessmen established in 1907 a commission to determine the origins of the game. Satisfied by the testimony of one Abner Graves, a schoolmate of Doubleday, the commission founded the National Baseball Hall of Fame at Cooperstown. Since that time, scholars have revealed that Doubleday was enrolled as a cadet at West Point in 1838 and probably never even visited Cooperstown. Nor does his published writing mention his alleged role in the creation of the game. Nevertheless, the legend has endured.

2. See Paul Hagen, "At 3rd, He's 2nd to None," *Philadelphia Daily News*, January 10, 1995; and Claire Smith, "Schmidt Puts Up Big Numbers Yet Again," *New York Times*, January 10, 1995; and Jerome Holtzman, "Mike Schmidt Joins Elite Hall of Fame Vote Leaders," *Baseball Digest* (April 1995): 21–22. Schmidt received 96.52 percent of the vote, making him the fourth highest vote-getter in history behind Tom Seaver (98.84 percent in 1992), Ty Cobb (98.23 percent in 1936) and Hank Aaron (97.83 percent in 1982).

3. See Bill Brown, "One Voice Against Schmidt," *Delaware County (Pa.) Daily Times*, January 10, 1995; and Brown, "A Dissenting Voice," *The Sporting News*, January 23, 1995. Bill Brown admitted that "if you go strictly by the numbers, there is no question at all about Schmidt's induction." Brown, however, contended that the rules governing enshrinement also state that "candidates shall be chosen on the basis of integrity, sportsmanship and character as well as playing ability." He proceeded to defame Schmidt as the "most arrogant, egomaniacal, and thoughtless player" he covered in his 11 years on the beat. Two years later, in a 1997 *Sports Illustrated* article titled "Joy Took A Backseat," former Phillies beat writer Michael Bamberger stated that Brown had prided himself in negativism and tearing down role models. According to Bamberger, Brown "decided who and what was cool" regarding Phillies baseball. Bamberger also claims that Brown "had no use for Mike Schmidt" because the third baseman "didn't dress in a manner acceptable to Brown, drive a car he approved of, listened to music he liked" and, most of all, because "religion mattered" to Schmidt.

4. Schmidt quoted in Frank Dolson, "In the Nick of Time, a Real Hero Arrives," *Philadelphia Inquirer*, January 11, 1998.

5. Ted Silary, "Schmidt and Ashburn Wow 'Em," *Philadelphia Daily News*, July 31, 1995. No previous induction day crowds had topped 20,000.

6. Excerpts of Schmidt's speech taken from "Schmidt: Cater to Fans," *Philadelphia Inquirer*, July 31, 1995.

7. Despite the ban, Mike remained close to his good friend, sharing the spotlight with him whenever possible. Perhaps he realized, deep down, that Rose's contributions may never be appropriately commemorated. In June 1991, for example, Rose made a surprise appearance at Reading Municipal Stadium, where Schmidt began his professional career. The Reading Phillies retired Schmidt's uniform number 24 on that occasion. It was questionable whether Rose's appearance at the ballpark violated the commissioner's ban. See Ted Silary, "Shades of the Past," *Philadelphia Daily News*, June 21, 1991; and "Rose Helps Reading Honor Mike Schmidt," *Philadelphia Inquirer*, June 21, 1991.

8. Ted Silary, "Rose Doesn't Stay for 'thank you,'" *Philadelphia Daily News*, July 31, 1995.

9. Ted Williams and Jim Price, *Ted Williams' Hit List* (Indianapolis: Masters, 1996), 139–41.

Epilogue

1. Schmidt interview, October 8, 1998, Jupiter, Florida.
2. *Ibid.*

Schmidt's Career Statistics

Michael Jack Schmidt. B. Sept. 27, 1949, Dayton, Ohio.
Hit right, threw right. Hall of Fame, 1995.

Year	Club	POS.	G	AB	R	H	2B	3B	HR	RBI	BA	SB	PO	A	E	FA
1971	Reading	SS-3B	74	237	27	50	7	1	8	31	.211		100	224	23	.934
1972	Eugene	2B-3B-SS	131	436	80	127	23	6	26	91	.291		271	324	25	.960
1972	Phila.	3B-2B	13	34	2	7	0	0	1	3	.206	0	10	25	2	.946
1973	Phila.	3B-2B-SS	132	367	43	72	11	0	18	52	.196	8	119	256	18	.954
1974	Phila.	3B	162	568	108	160	28	7	36	116	.282	23	134	404	26	.954
1975	Phila.	3B-SS	158	562	93	140	34	3	38	95	.249	29	139	390	26	.953
1976	Phila.	3B	160	584	112	153	31	4	38	107	.262	14	139	377	21	.961
1977	Phila.	3B-SS-2B	154	544	114	149	27	11	38	101	.274	15	109	401	20	.962
1978	Phila.	3B-SS	145	513	93	129	27	2	21	78	.251	19	98	325	16	.964
1979	Phila.	3B-SS	160	541	109	137	25	4	45	114	.253	9	115	363	23	.954
1980	Phila.	3B	150	548	104	157	25	8	48	121	.286	12	98	372	27	.946
1981	Phila.	3B	102	354	78	112	19	2	31	91	.316	12	74	249	15	.956
1982	Phila.	3B	148	514	108	144	26	3	35	87	.280	14	110	324	23	.950
1983	Phila.	3B-SS	154	534	104	136	16	4	40	109	.255	7	108	333	19	.959
1984	Phila.	3B-1B-SS	151	528	93	146	23	3	36	106	.277	5	93	330	26	.942
1985	Phila.	1B-3B-SS	158	549	89	152	31	5	33	93	.277	1	911	193	18	.984
1986	Phila.	3B-1B	160	552	97	160	29	1	37	119	.290	1	347	238	8	.987
1987	Phila.	3B-1B-SS	147	522	88	153	28	0	35	113	.293	2	138	319	13	.972
1988	Phila.	3B-1B	108	390	52	97	21	2	12	62	.251	3	76	223	19	.940
1989	Phila.	3B	42	148	19	30	7	0	6	28	.203	0	18	71	8	.918
Major League Totals—18 yrs:			2404	8352	1496	2234	408	59	548	1595	.267	174	2836	5193	328	.961

Championship Series Record

Year	POS.	G	AB	R	H	2B	3B	HR	RBI	BA	PO	A	E	FA
1976	3B	3	13	1	4	2	0	0	2	.308	4	9	1	.929
1977	3B	4	16	2	1	0	0	0	1	.063	4	15	0	1.000
1978	3B	4	15	1	3	2	0	0	1	.200	3	18	2	.913
1980	3B	5	24	1	5	1	0	0	1	.208	3	17	1	.952
1983	3B	4	15	5	7	2	0	1	2	.467	6	7	1	.929
Totals—5 yrs:		20	83	10	20	7	0	1	7	.241	20	66	5	.945

World Series Record

Year	POS.	G	AB	R	H	2B	3B	HR	RBI	BA	PO	A	E	FA
1980	3B	6	21	6	8	1	0	2	7	.381	9	8	0	1.000
1983	3B	5	20	0	1	0	0	0	0	.050	1	10	1	.917
Totals—2yrs.:		11	41	6	9	1	0	2	7	.220	10	18	1	.966

Schmidt's Career Achievements

Elected to the National Baseball Hall of Fame: 1995

Named Baseball "Player of the Decade" for the 1980s
by *The Sporting News*

World Series Most Valuable Player: 1980

National League Most Valuable Player (three years): 1980, 1981, 1986

The Sporting News' Player of the Year (two years): 1980, 1986

National League Home Run Champion (eight years):
1974, 1975, 1976, 1980, 1981, 1983, 1984, 1986

548 career home runs (seventh all-time)

Home run ratio of 1 every 15.26 at-bats (fifth best all-time)

National League RBI Champion (four years): 1980, 1981, 1984, 1986

1,595 RBI (seventeenth all-time)

Gold Glove Award Winner (ten years): 1976–1984, 1986

National League All-Star (12 years): 1974, 1976,
1977, 1979–84, 1986–87, 1989*

(*First player ever voted to the All-Star Team after his retirement)

Voted Greatest Phillies Player of All-Time

Holds 24 Phillies career records

1983 Recipient of the Lou Gehrig Award, given to the
major league player who best exemplifies Gehrig's
personal character and playing ability

Selected Bibliography

Four books had been written about Mike Schmidt's life prior to the present work: *Mike Schmidt: The Human Vacuum Cleaner* by Mike Herbert; *Mike Schmidt: Baseball's King of Swing* by Stan Hochman; *Mike Schmidt: Baseball Legend* by Rich Westcott; and *Mike Schmidt: Baseball's Young Lion* by Jim Wright. All of these treatments are children's literature. Schmidt himself coauthored two books that deal, indirectly, with his life: *Always on the Offense*, with Barbara Walder, and *The Mike Schmidt Study: Hitting Theory, Skills and Technique*, with Rob Ellis.

He has postponed the writing of an autobiography, having been discouraged by the explosion of kiss-and-tell biographies that have scandalized the sport over the last decade (see Schmidt quoted in *USA Today*, July 14, 1989). It is hoped he will soon author a book about his life and career, which influenced some of the major patterns in the game, including free agency, the business aspects of baseball, and the changing role of sports heroes.

Contemporary periodicals composed the major source for this book. Among the best of these sources were *The Philadelphia Inquirer*, *The Philadelphia Daily News* and *The Sporting News*. Below are listed those primary and secondary sources I found most helpful. The bibliography does not represent an exhaustive list of sources, but provides a starting point for those who would like to pursue the various topics addressed in this book.

Allen, Dick, and Tim Whitaker. *Crash: The Life and Times of Dick Allen* (New York: Ticknor and Fields, 1989).

Bowa, Larry, with Barry Bloom. *Bleep! Larry Bowa Manages* (Chicago: Bonus Books, 1988).

Bowden, Mark. "The Short, Sad Spring of Michael Schmidt," *Philadelphia Inquirer Magazine* (May 16, 1982).

Brown, Bill. "Schmidt Selected TSN Player of the Decade." *The Sporting News* (January 29, 1990): 9–11.

Deford, Frank. "Religion in Sports" *Sports Illustrated* (a three-part series: April 19, 26, and May 3, 1976).

Dolson, Frank. *Beating the Bushes: Life in the Minor Leagues* (South Bend, IN: Icarus, 1982).

_____. "How Pete Rose Helped Nudge Mike Schmidt to Greatness," *Baseball Digest* (May 1995): 61–62.

Falls, Joe. "God and the Gladiators: More and More Athletes Turn to Religion," *Parade Magazine* (April 23, 1978): 1–4.

Herbert, Mike. *Mike Schmidt: The Human Vacuum Cleaner* (Chicago:Children's Press, 1983).

Hochman, Stan. *Mike Schmidt: Baseball's King of Swing* (New York: Random House, 1983).

Honig, Donald. *The Philadelphia Phillies: An Illustrated History* (New York: Simon and Schuster, 1992).

_____. *The Power Hitters* (St. Louis: The Sporting News, 1989).

Hubbard, Steve. *Faith in Sports: Athletes and Their Religion On and Off the Field* (New York: Doubleday, 1998).

Kaplan, Jim. "Third Is the Word," *Sports Illustrated* (April 13, 1981): 20–26.

Keith, Larry. "It's Either a Clout or an Out," *Sports Illustrated* (May 3, 1976): 20–22.

Kuenster, Bob. "All-Time Best Third Basemen Starred as Hitters, Fielders," *Baseball Digest* (September 1994): 32–38.

Kuenster, John. "Farewell to Mike Schmidt, One of Game's All Time Great Third Basemen," *Baseball Digest* (September 1989): 15–17.

"Legends in Their Own Time. Mike Schmidt and Rich Ashburn," *The Philadelphia Daily News* (keepsake edition), July 26, 1995.

Lewis, Allen. *The Philadelphia Phillies: A Pictorial History* (Virginia Beach: JCP, 1981).

Pascarelli, Peter. "Mike Schmidt: Staying Power," *The Sporting News* (March 30, 1987): 11–12.

The Philadelphia Daily News, 1973–1995.

The Philadelphia Inquirer, 1973–1995.

Platt, Larry. "The Unloved: Mike Schmidt," *Philadelphia Magazine* (July 1995): 53–56, 81–82.

Rieland, Randy. *Baseball in the 1970s: The New Professionals* (Alexandria, VA: Redefinition, 1989).

Rose, Pete, and Roger Kahn. *Pete Rose: My Story* (New York: Macmillan, 1989).

Rosenberg, Barry. "Two for the See-Saw: Mike Schmidt and Dick Allen," *Philadelphia Magazine* (September 1975): 130–44.

Searcy, Jay. "The Transfiguration of Mike Schmidt," *Philadelphia Inquirer Magazine* (October 26, 1986): 12–18.

Schmidt, Mike. "Pride of the Philadelphia Phillies: An Interview with Mike Schmidt," by William C. Kashatus. *Pennsylvania Heritage* (Fall 1995): 12–19.

_____. "Something More," *Guideposts* (July 1987): 3–5.

_____, with Rob Ellis. *The Mike Schmidt Study: Hitting Theory, Skills and Technique* (Atlanta: McGriff and Bell, Inc., 1994).

_____, with Barbara Walder. *Always on the Offense* (New York: Atheneum, 1982).

Schoor, Gene. *The History of the World Series* (New York: William Morrow, 1990).

Shatzkin, Mike. *The Ball Players: Baseball's Ultimate Reference Book* (New York: William Morrow, 1990).

Smith, Chris. "God Is an .800 Hitter," *New York Times Magazine* (July 27, 1997): 26–32.

Thorn, John, and Pete Palmer. *Total Baseball* (New York: Warner, 1989).

Vass, George. "Talent Explosion at the 'Hot Corner,'" *Baseball Digest* (May 1975): 20–24.

Weingardner, Mark. *Prophet of the Sandlots: Journeys with a Major League Scout* (New York: Atlantic Monthly Press, 1990).

Westcott, Rich. *Mike Schmidt: Baseball Legend* (Philadelphia: Chelsea House, 1995).

_____, and Frank Bilovsky. *The New Phillies Encyclopedia* (Philadelphia: Temple University Press, 1993).

Wolff, Rick, editor. *The Baseball Encyclopedia* (8th edition) (New York: Macmillan, 1990).

Wright, Jim. *Mike Schmidt: Baseball's Young Lion* (New York: Putnam, 1979).

Yagoda, Ben. "What's the Big Deal," *Philly Sport* (July 1989): 30–35.

Index